Stamford '76

Stamford '76

A TRUE STORY OF MURDER, CORRUPTION, RACE, AND FEMINISM IN THE 1970S

JoeAnn Hart

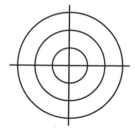

UNIVERSITY OF IOWA PRESS, IOWA CITY

University of Iowa Press, Iowa City 52242

Copyright © 2019 by JoeAnn Hart

www.uipress.uiowa.edu

Printed in the United States of America

Design by April Leidig

Printed on acid-free paper

Library of Congress Cataloging-in-Publication Data
Names: Hart, JoeAnn, author.
Title: Stamford '76 : a true story of murder, corruption, race,
    and feminism in the 1970s / By JoeAnn Hart.
Description: Iowa City : University of Iowa Press, [2019] |
    Includes index. |

Identifiers: LCCN 2018044534 (print) | LCCN 2018046552 (ebook) |
    ISBN 978-1-60938-638-2 | ISBN 978-1-60938-637-5 (pbk. : alk. paper)
Subjects: LCSH: Olson, Margo, 1951–1976. | Hart, JoeAnn. | Murder—
    Connecticut—Stamford—Case studies. | Police corruption—
    Connecticut—Stamford—Case studies. | Stamford (Conn.)—Race
    relations—History—20th century. | Stamford (Conn.)—Social
    conditions—20th century.
Classification: LCC HV6534.S675 (ebook) | LCC HV6534.S675 H37 2019 (print) |
    DDC 364.152/3092—dc23
LC record available at https://lccn.loc.gov/2018044534

KATA TON DAIMONA EAYTOY

While our bodies move ever forward on the time line, our minds continuously trace backward, seeking shape and meaning as deftly as any arrow seeking its mark.
—Lucy Grealy, *Autobiography of a Face*

Acknowledgments

MANY THANKS to all those who revisited difficult days so that I could know Margo as they did. Ilene Lush, I'm looking at you. You too, Pam. To the Raymond Street Writers who endured several versions of the manuscript, and Maxine Rodburg and Catherine Parnell, who were so generous with advice and support, I love you all. A big hug to Lauren MacLeod for believing. Special thanks to John Breunig and Zach Lowe of the Stamford *Advocate*, who opened many doors, as well as the librarians at the Ferguson Library who walked me through others. I could not have begun this book if it hadn't been for George Packer, who asked the critical early questions, and I would not have finished it without James McCoy and the insightful team at the University of Iowa Press, who asked the later ones. For my family, as always, thank you for your patience.

Introduction

"SOMETHING FOUL" was in the air, and the ominous stench put a quick end to the morning's fun. On July 14, 1976, six years after Stamford's potter's field was abandoned by the city and the land had become choked with bracken and vine, a high school teacher took his mom and a cousin on a hunt for lost grave markers. And they were just that. Markers. No names, no dates, only numbers chiseled on gray stones set into the dirt like those used to indicate property lines. But it was Stamford history all the same, and somewhere, I'm guessing, secreted in the basement of the historical society, sits a moldering book wherein those numbers reveal the stories of the dead.

I understand the appeal a place like the potter's field had for this family. I am drawn to old graveyards myself. My daughter jokes that when we went to Paris in 2006, we spent more time tracking down Jim Morrison's littered slab in Père Lachaise cemetery than we spent at the Louvre.

"What's your point?" I asked her, but I knew the point. I've always liked to view the past through the prism of something physical and weighted with meaning, something like a grave.

On the morning of the Stamford field trip, it was not just hot, it was steamy. It had been showering off and on for more than a week without ever drying out, making for an oppressive day. The air had weight. Mosquitoes drifted in search of a blood meal and storm clouds gathered on the horizon, but the teacher and his family paid them no mind. Curious about what they might discover, they were cheerfully absorbed in their investigation, tramping through the overgrown landscape, calling out discoveries and moving dank brush aside with their hands, until, with a start, they recoiled at the first whiff of decay. The teacher, a bit apprehensively no doubt, followed the odor into a cedar thicket, where their worst fears were made fact. An animal, grubbing for meat, had scratched around a shallowly interred corpse, exposing an arm and the top of a foot, both streaked with green and black, the colors of late-stage rot.

For exactly one hundred years, the potter's field had been the dumping ground for Stamford's indigent, unclaimed, or unidentified bodies. Whatever their lives might have been before, whatever their age, gender, or color of their skin, in the end they were all roughly discarded by some city worker. The bodies were thrown together, one on top of another, sometimes without so much as a box. Criminals and the young were often just wrapped in cloth and lowered into the earth. The first shovel of dirt was lifted in 1870, soon after the Civil War, and the last mound was tamped down in 1970, when the field closed. Maybe the plot was finally full to overflowing. More likely, the law changed and the city was allowed to cremate the bodies instead, an option that took up no real estate at all. The graveyard, such as it was, fell into neglect, and because of its isolation it became both a druggie hangout and a lover's lane, a place of potential danger in either case. The police did not patrol the area. As for me, I never visited the field during the two years I lived in Connecticut, and for that much I am grateful.

Before the body in the potter's field had a name, the coroner at the next day's autopsy estimated that the white female had been dead for more than ten days. A final meal of fried chicken and coleslaw was still in her stomach. And even though the police, insect-like in their gas masks, had originally reported no signs of foul play when they exhumed her, the coroner found an arrowhead used for hunting big game piercing her heart.

A bow and arrow is a weapon powered by the tension between two opposing forces. The farther the clenched fists push forward and pull back, the more energy is released in the form of an arrow and the greater the penetration into the mark. In this case, the arrowhead was buried so deep the killer couldn't pull it out. The shaft was snapped off inside the ribs, which means someone had walked away from the body clutching a jagged stick with heart tissue still clinging to it. After an anonymous tip to the police, days after the body was found, Margo Olson was identified by dental records and claimed by her mother.

When this news first appeared in the paper in July 1976, I stared at it in horror and could hardly comprehend the words. I only knew Margo at the end of her short life, her last year, when she seemed to be falling apart, and yet her death produced such fear that I promptly buried her and put her out of my mind. Decades later, just at the point I had trouble even recalling her name, her death slowly became as vivid to me as if she had just been murdered. It took that long for the words to sink in. It took much longer to understand my fear. Since then, I have tried to gently brush the dirt off her face with my hand to get a better look, contemplating the shape of her hurried grave and wondering what brought her to that place. But I can only follow her back to a certain point, and she can never follow me here. I doubt that she would want to come with me if she could. She would not want to leave the one she loved.

It took time, but after sifting through the disturbed earth for so long, I can now envision the tall, striking young woman Margo had been. Growing up in Darien,* a top-shelf community abutting Stamford to the east, she'd been a Girl Scout, taught Sunday school, and sang in the church choir. When her parents divorced, her father retreated to Kentucky and Margo seemed to show no regret. At the time of her death, her mother had remarried and was living a few miles away in Wilton, another affluent town. By all accounts from those who knew Margo in Darien high school, she was a smart, artistic student who loved backgammon and played a decent game of tennis. There was always what a friend called "a certain sadness" about her. After high school, she went to Fairleigh Dickinson University in New Jersey, where she graduated with a degree in childhood education.

All in all, she seemed an unlikely candidate to end up as a body dump. But she, like so many other young women at the time—women like me—had wandered off the main road searching for something we couldn't even name. We were inchoate desire and just hoped we'd know what we were looking for when we found it.

Margo and I met in the fall of 1975, when I was eighteen and she was twenty-four. My first impression was that she looked like Janis Joplin, so recently deceased, with a soft, suspicious face that peered through a curtain of peachy hair. Margo didn't talk so much as mumble, making it hard to tell whether she was trying to communicate with me or with someone in her head. She dropped acid on a regular basis, so it was unclear whether her strangeness was a result of drugs, or whether she was self-medicating a legacy of preexisting problems. Outside her boyfriend's circle, of which I stood on the periphery, she had, like me, few friends of her own in Stamford. It was not our town. Margo was just that much older, and just this side of

*Nicknamed Aryan Darien, it was the setting for the 1947 Gregory Peck movie *Gentleman's Agreement* about an anti-Semitic community.

odd, so she was not someone I would have known if I had not been living with Joe Louis, who was friends with her boyfriend, Howie Carter. Howie and Margo were another interracial couple in town, like us. Both men were black, both women white. Howie was a suspect in Margo's murder but was never charged. He did not leave town. He did not run. A few weeks later he was shot and killed by the police.

America's bicentennial was a time of renewed reverence for the past. In that spirit, Joe created our own history for 1976, but it's proved to be an unconvincing narrative. The story that I bought from Joe was that the police, who in Joe's lights were capable of any atrocity, did not have the evidence to convict a presumably innocent Howie for Margo's death, so they killed him instead, and—like everything else in Joe's black-and-white world—it was racially motivated. And who can say he was wrong about that? Not me. Not by a long shot. But Joe never addressed the issue of who might have plunged the arrow in Margo's heart, as if her death were a mere accessory to Howie's wrongful one, and I never asked.

I never asked.

To be fair, and I want very much to be fair, I was the one who read what I wanted into the story. If prejudice means to prejudge, then I stand as guilty as anyone else. I made assumptions. Race was a red herring that dragged my attention away from Margo's murder back to the unjust society we lived in, a jagged hole of racial tension so big it could suck up something the size of a dead body and make it disappear. I was wrapped in a shroud of oblivion and privilege I had stitched by hand. Even to wonder aloud who might have killed Margo seemed a dangerous misstep at the time. The arrow pointed both ways, at the woman who lay half buried in the underbrush, then back at me.

In a vivid dream I had early in the long writing of this book, I was getting a psychic reading. The psychic, an older woman, had a handheld device that she claimed was going to reveal a number to help with the reading. The numbers on the screen whizzed by in a blur, one after another like the years, and then a message appeared. The psychic said that a dead woman wanted to communicate with me, was that okay? I said sure, thinking the psychic would channel her, but I was the one who started speaking for the dead, screaming "Go away, leave me alone," over and over. I woke up with my heart pounding somewhere on the other side of the room.

PART 1

The unsupported word of a witness who
was not present except in imagination
would not be acceptable in a court of law,
but, as it has been demonstrated over and
over, the sworn testimony of the witness
who was present is not trustworthy either.

—William Maxwell,
So Long, See You Tomorrow

*I*T WAS IN THE SPRING OF 1999, during the-end-of-the-world-as-we-know-it buildup to the millennium, when time and its significant markers were much on the collective mind, that I started thinking about writing a short piece about Howie and Margo. Armed with a quiver full of justice and indignation, I was going to reveal long-buried truths about their deaths, and with them, the underground streams of institutionalized racism and police malfeasance that once seeped through Stamford like a broken sewer. My essay was going to expose Howie and Margo's story to the cleansing light of the written word. It was going to be cut and dried, black and white, and it was going to have nothing whatsoever to do with me. That was my mission.

Well, we all know what happens to missionaries.

The story nearly ate me alive.

I opened up a Word document and titled it "Stamford." Then, just as I was about to start writing about Howie's death at the hands of the police, I realized, with some surprise, that I didn't know who killed Margo. And I couldn't write about Howie's violent end without first addressing hers. I presumed that her bizarre murder, certainly by some random maniac, had been solved, and I had somehow forgotten the outcome or had never been told. So I picked up the phone and called my cousin Denise.

The decade of our coming of age—our teens and early twenties—not the one of our birth, makes for a generation, so that placed me and Denise squarely in the 70s. We'd rather have been members of the 60s, but we were just kids then, watching our older cousins and their friends live out the psychedelic dream in our aunt's basement. We'd hide at the bottom of the stairs in a trance, listening to our cousin Michael's band render Donovan's "Season of the Witch" unrecognizable, as we gazed wistfully up an imaginary road. The air smelled of pot, tobacco, and incense. The clothes were soft and loose, the feet bare. We closed our eyes and divined the future, a utopian world of pleasure and possibility. Even though Aunt Ginny had just the one child, who died in 1981 in a motorcycle accident, there was always a bedraggled soul or two on her sofa. Sometimes these were other cousins seeking a respite from their own families, but usually they were local teens who had run away from home, often just blocks away, looking to divest themselves of a middle-class existence in search of life's truths.

Yes, I thought, yes. There was more to the world than what I could see in the suburban culture around me, which seemed materially bland and spiritually bereft. I was particularly fascinated with the longhaired boys who espoused a litany of freedom, justice, and rebellion. It never sunk into my tie-dyed brain that they might only be playing at being rebels, or that there was something particularly privileged about the renunciation of privilege. Most never got farther than Aunt Ginny's sofa.

During the time I was with Joe, Denise had been my steady—and at times only—connection to my family. She'd take the train up from the Bronx, where she lived, to visit me and Joe in Stamford, then later in Westport. I told her everything, so I thought finding out about Margo would be as simple as a telephone call, as if I were retrieving information I had put into storage. Even then, even with decades of stability padding my bones, with marriage, three children, and a home hundreds of miles away from Stamford, I was uneasy.

Funny, I thought to myself. It was as if I didn't really want to know what happened.

It was no coincidence that I decided to find out about Margo just as my two girls and a boy were creeping closer to the age I was when I met Joe. When my oldest daughter started acting out in the predictable ways of adolescence, I flashed back to Margo's piteous end. Danger, danger, the alarms rang in my head, but what was there in their pampered lives for me to fear? They'd been shielded from every imaginable threat since birth, bound in car seats, topped with bicycle helmets, and slathered in 35 SPF sunscreen to protect their fair skin, and yet I knew, deep down, I was helpless to protect them from the unimaginable dangers, the ones where young women ended up as body dumps by the side of the road. The zeal I had devoted to grinding organic carrots for baby food had only been a talismanic rite to keep that other world at bay. As my girls began to maneuver the adolescent tightwire of freedom and responsibility, I saw myself in their struggle to come to terms with what it means to be female in a world that, even after decades of feminism, can feel as if we're peddling backward. If I could not figure out how Margo ended up in the potter's field, how would I know what the path looked like so I could place a Jersey barrier across it for my children? That seems like an absurd leap to make, but anyone who has raised a fourteen-year-old girl has experienced the kind of stress that can make a mother daft with paranoia.

A small lump settled in my chest as I dialed Denise, and every ring on the other end of the line made me want to bail. I had to force myself to keep the receiver to my ear. What was I so afraid of? At the sound of her voice, I shot out the question, as if it had been under pressure.

"Who killed Margo?"

"Are you shitting me?" she said, without missing a beat, not in the least bit surprised to hear Margo's name mentioned for the first time in decades, as if she'd been sitting by the phone all that time waiting for me to call. "Howie killed her. Of all people you should know that. He told you at a card game that if he was going to kill anyone it would be with a bow and arrow."

GAMBLING DENS. I don't know what else to call them. What word is there to describe a residential basement or garage with a card table set up for a few handles of booze and a single round table for playing cards? Joe and I went to these places once in a while, mostly just to watch good poker while we sipped cheap scotch. Joe's mother, Georgia, had taught me to drink scotch after hearing me order a sloe gin fizz at a bar. "You've got to have a grown-up drink, sugar," and changed my order to a Dewar's with a splash and a twist, "just like at the Peppermint Lounge,"* where she once sang backup for Ray Charles.

This particular garage in Stamford was no Peppermint Lounge.* The clientele was all black men with the occasional white girlfriend, like me. I could not have imagined that what I saw was only the tip of a much bigger iceberg of gambling in Stamford, black or white. It was truly an equal opportunity enterprise. Sometimes I played. They called me the White House and let me win a hand so I'd bet more and lose it all. Joe knew the game. He smiled at my first hand when I'd looked at him so proudly, then laughed at my second. I've never seen a man who loved to lose as much as he did. Howie was on my left (Where was Margo? He never seemed to go anywhere with Margo),

*A popular discotheque in New York City from 1958 to 1965, where the twist and go-go dancing originated.

sitting on a stool, looking down at his cards and saying that if he was going to kill someone—God knows how table talk had turned to *that*—it would be with a bow and arrow. It was my turn to laugh. There was so much male bravado around me, there was no taking any of it seriously.

———————————

IF I WERE READING a murder mystery, and the protagonist heard the words, "If I were going to kill someone it would be with a bow and arrow," from this Howie character, then wondered out loud a few pages later who might have killed his girlfriend with a bow and arrow, I'd close the book. No reasonable person could refuse to put such obvious pieces together. But what does reason have to do with fear? Think of obliviousness as the bubble pack of life. It kept me from breaking in transit. With no self-awareness whatsoever, I had stored Margo's arrow-pierced body where I couldn't get at her. It's not that I didn't remember Howie's telling me about his murder weapon of choice, once Denise reminded me what I already knew, it was that, unlike Denise, my younger self had failed to connect that information to the fact of Margo's death. Or if I had made the connection, I promptly severed the line. There was something about her death that went beyond reason, refusing to find a settled place in the past.

To fully grasp how disturbing my own memories were to my conscious mind, consider this. The first time I made a stab at putting words on paper about Margo and Howie, I wrote a few pages, condensing their story into the basic elements of what I knew. I could feel my heart beating in my fingertips the whole time I was typing, perhaps an hour, and I was relieved when it was done. A first draft. When I read it through, I thought I had done a good job of capturing the essence of what had happened. Then, on the second reading, I realized I had left out that Margo had been killed too, not just Howie. I smiled to myself, shook my head, and put it aside.

What else didn't I remember or just outright block out? I didn't know Margo that well to begin with, and it was clear from the card game episode that I had a fairly warped memory of anything in her orbit. If I was going to write about her, I couldn't rely on what was in my head. If I wanted to find out how she died, I'd have to ask the questions I had failed to ask back then. And even though I began this project determined to keep myself out of it, I kept turning to my younger self and asking, "Well, what did *you* think?" But I couldn't hear her. I could barely even see her, the thin girl with straight brown hair, the serious gray eyes that would not return my gaze. Leaving behind the memory of Margo had meant forgetting parts of myself, and I needed that eighteen-year-old by my side as I faced the challenge of getting three children through their teenage years. I wanted to gain some wisdom from that girl, who was both brave and reckless to a fault, and to do that, I had to open the box marked Fragile. In that box, nestled along with all my stored emotion, was a three-pronged mission: (1) figure out what had happened to Margo, (2) remember what had been going on with me, and (3) try to understand why her death made me so wary, for so long.

Finding Margo seemed, at least at first, to be fairly straightforward. I relied on the archives of the Stamford *Advocate*, which, aside from shedding a light on the world I lived in, had the newspaper accounts of her death as well as Howie's. Through Joe, I knew Howie well enough, Margo, much less so. I didn't even know who Margo's friends were. I tried to find as many people as Joe and I knew back then, but I never knew the last names of many of them to begin with. It was an enormous help to discover that Joe had written a novel using everyone's real names, more or less. Another book, *Rogue Town* by Vito Colucci, a nonfiction account of the 1970s Stamford Police Department, was useful as well. The internet was fairly primitive when I started this project, but even as it matured, many people have remained elusive. Some have died. Others, like Margo's family, did not want to talk. Howie's family did not want to talk.

I am no investigative reporter, so I cop to the plea of not really knowing what I was doing most of the time. For instance, I did not know that regular people could employ the Freedom of Information Act to obtain criminal files and relied instead on a reporter who was able to access Margo's murder file at the police station. Each step forward in Margo's death took time. Each step triggered an overhaul of the story, which often made me put the project aside until I could wrap my head around any ill-fitting revelations.

Finding me required less research but more soul searching. I had to read between the lines, looking hard at what I had suppressed and why. I listened to the things I did not say, watched what I did not do. I looked at how I neatly packed up Margo's death and stored it away. I compared historical fact to my memory of events. At times I questioned history, other times my self. I had to reexamine my attitudes about race and white privilege, then and now. I had entered my relationship with Joe with expectations I didn't know I carried. On some unarticulated level, I was drawn to the idea of me and Joe as some manifestation of equality, both gender and racial. There we were after all, black and white, man and woman, side by side. The racial seems self-evident—but gender? Logic has never been idealism's strong suit. Every time I'd pointed out some inequity in our relationship to Joe, something as basic as who had first dibs on the car, he said, "What are you going to do? Call NOW?" as he drove away, laughing. He thought the National Organization of Women was a joke, and feminism itself hysterically funny.

It wasn't funny. It was nothing less than self-determination. It's what, in the end, we were all after. Me, Margo, Howie, Joe. We wanted equality. We wanted justice. We wanted to not be controlled by the world as it was.

*I*N THE FRAMEWORK of this narrative, Stamford serves as both the landscape and the backstory. It supplies the plot and the atmosphere. It does everything but fondle the murder weapon. Such a major player needs its own introduction. Not as it is now. What it is now is so different from what it was in the mid-70s, it is as if it had gone into the witness protection program and come out with a fake passport and a nylon wig. HUD, the U.S. Department of Housing and Urban Development, was responsible in the 60s and 70s for what was called urban renewal but really meant urban removal. By the time I arrived, Stamford's rubble had already been bulldozed, loaded into trucks, and hauled away to be dumped as fill.

The city was starting fresh, just like me. It was, as a whole, an unpromising time in which to start a life, not just in Connecticut but anywhere in the country. States and municipalities were failing left and right. Garbage was piling up all over the country because cities couldn't afford to have it picked up. The post office wanted to cut mail delivery to three days a week. When I was growing up in Bronx and then Westchester, New York was like the sun, supplying light, heat, and gravity to all the bodies in its orbit, but by the 70s, this sun was eclipsed by blight and decay. White flight had taken so much of New York's tax base that in October 1975 Mayor Abe Beame had to ask for a bailout from President Ford.

*Ford to City: Drop Dead.**

Ford, who had just survived two assassination attempts—one woman hoping to gain the approval of mass murderer Charles Manson, the other woman just trying to effect change—would blame losing the general election

Daily News, October 29, 1975.

to Carter in November 1976 on that headline. He had only narrowly edged out Ronald Reagan at the Republican Convention, but Reagan would be back before the 70s were over. Ford didn't even say "Drop Dead." He swears. It was the *Daily News* manipulating his words and manipulating the story. Because in the end, Ford did bail out the city.

Thank you, Mr. President, but even with the bailout, it was too little, too late. New York City corporations scattered like cockroaches. Families like mine had left the Bronx and settled in quaint suburban villages, but corporations needed somewhat more infrastructure than a septic tank and a municipal pool. They're not corporations for nothing. They wanted things. Land for one—lots of it—not to mention transportation, schools, housing, and labor.

Stamford frantically waved its hand. The city council wanted those taxes. The developers, realtors, and merchants needed those corporations because they weren't feeling too well themselves. Everyone had some skin in the game. *Please.* We are the perfect city. We have already razed the unsightly downtown (read: black community) using HUD money. Gone! A white slate! Do us. Here is Interstate-95 slicing through the midsection, making it highly commutable from just about everywhere. A straight shot. The city also had the Merritt Parkway in North Stamford, a curvaceous road that rubbed thighs with Greenwich, ideal for executives already living there. If they moved their businesses to Stamford, their commutes would be a roll out of bed. If only I-95 had easy exits for the workers to hop on and off. The city fathers wrung their hands.

There was endless backroom wrestling. There were negotiations with the powers that be in D.C. and Hartford, and with the powers that lurk beneath the surface of respectability. Promises. Deals. More deals. Stamford got its fancy-pants exits. This improved transportation cost millions and millions. Nice! Corporations started sniffing around and everyone was rubbing their hands together. There was that newly leveled downtown, ready for anything. The F. D. Rich Company, the city-designated urban renewal developer, had done the leveling. The company was founded by Grandpa Rich, an Italian immigrant who arrived in the city as a stonemason and presumably shortened his last name at the gate—or changed it altogether. In one generation his company won the one-hundred-million-dollar HUD contract to revitalize 130 acres of downtown Stamford. The American Dream. In North Stamford, where the land was not cluttered with unsightly human habitation, F. D. was playing around with the fresh concept of the corporate park up on High Ridge Road. In the pit of the recession, future prosperity was in the air.

As the old Stamford was being consigned to the scrap heap, the new one was trying to poke out through the debris. The twenty-two-story One Landmark Square was designed to be accessible only by car to deter crime. Built in 1973, it still seemed uninhabited when I got there. The new GTE building, an upside-down Mayan ruin, was a curiosity, but again, a tad lifeless. The paint was barely dry on the Marriott Hotel, which had a revolving restaurant on top and was integral to F. D.'s redevelopment plan as a place to entertain and house corporate prospects. And then there were St. John's Towers, low-income housing developments in the shape of three trash cans, where the old downtown residents (read: black residents) had been dumped. The towers themselves came into being as the result of a lawsuit in the early 70s that stopped Stamford's urban renewal because it had destroyed nine hundred downtown housing units without replacing a single one. F. D. fought the towers every inch of the way. There's no profit in housing low-income families, but if he wanted to continue the flow of federal money, he had to build them. They were, for a time, distinctive features of the city skyline.

Yet when I arrived in 1975, for all this activity and promise, Stamford looked dead in the water. HUD was taking a breath to question the wisdom of clear-cutting homes, and as it paused, what was left of the city began to burn, one fire after another. What the HUD-financed bulldozers did not destroy, fires took care of. It seemed that instead of zoning waivers and building permits and all that silly red tape, the fastest path to a new Stamford was with a match. Downtown was scorched earth. An entire shopping center in the business district was left in cinders, and the fire inspectors just shrugged. The department also shrugged off being sued in October 1975 for violating the civil rights of blacks and minorities in hiring (three black members out of 206, no Hispanics). The city made no effort to set things right, although the finance board did fret mightily over what effect the suit would have on their bond rating.

———————

TODAY, DRIVING THROUGH the city on I-95, Stamford presents a concrete wall of a shopping complex to the world, giving it the medieval quality of a fortress.* Rising behind the wall are financial cathedrals of skyscraper glass and sharp edges, with an alphabet of corporate names, USB, RBS, shorthand

*According to F. D. Rich: "GTE came here because they were bombed in New York. Crime was a problem in the city. That's why the buildings were designed to be impenetrable."

for money. It is the future the city dreamed of back in the 70s, a goal relentlessly pursued, with fortunes made as quickly as buildings could tumble or burn. It is physically transformed beyond recognition, but demographically it is not so very different. In 1976, Stamford had a population of more than 100,000, with 13 percent black and a couple more percentage points Hispanic. Now it is around 131,000, making it the third largest city in Connecticut instead of the fourth. The population is just over 50% white, 24% Hispanic, 8% Asian, and still 13% black, with many people of color foreign-born. The largest industry is now financial services, but in the 70s Stamford was still clinging to an industrial economy, including boat building, an activity that blocked access to the Long Island Sound. Except for the few times I was out on Shippan Point, a wealthy residential neighborhood, I was barely aware that we were on the coast. There was a grungy but serviceable area of downtown that had survived fire and demolition, with a Bloomingdale's and a Caldor's, along with some small shops and restaurants that catered to a lackluster business scene. But head north from downtown Stamford, and it was—and still is—like driving into a New England postcard of reforested pasture. Nestled in this bucolic world, just north of the Merritt, is the potter's field. It was still very much an active burial ground when Joe and Howie were growing up. It would have been a common fact of their childhood that on the edge of the city was a space reserved for the poor or unclaimed dead. It is not inconceivable, in fact, it is probable, that they would have known some of the buried residents. Stamford was their town.

*I*T WAS IN THE pinkish-gray divide of the day that I first laid eyes on Joe. I was eighteen years old, serving pitchers and counting dimes at the Blue Note Café. I had been working there for about two weeks, which was just a few days longer than I had lived in Stamford. I had just dropped out of Skidmore College after a single year. Used to nuns or parents telling me what I should feel and think, college felt vaguely unsatisfying because it didn't assume to tell me what to do, it just displayed the menu. For an art history major, that menu was filtered through a Renaissance painting, and I could not see what it had to do with my life. I do now, but I didn't then. Instead of trying to figure it out, and tired of listening to my parents complain about how much college cost after my father was briefly without a job, I did not reenroll. I wanted to step into an authentic life with meaning and purpose, although I had only a shadowy idea of what that might be.

Without much forethought, knowing only that I needed to get out of Pleasantville, I agreed to find a place with another Skidmore dropout, Christie, who grew up in Old Greenwich, the town next to Stamford. After our summer jobs ended, we packed up our existential misery, and with a few boxes of clothes and records, we moved on September 1, 1975. It was International Women's Year. Our post-Nixon president, Gerald Ford, called for the ratification of the Equal Rights Amendment (thank you, Betty), and the National Organization for Women organized the first Take Back the Night to bring attention to sexual violence against women. Ella Grasso was the governor of Connecticut, the first elected woman governor in America. Women were running for office all over the country, breaking barriers and assuming power in business as well as government. Feminism had expanded our notions of what was possible, and Christie and I wanted to see what those possibilities looked like in the real world. Why we thought that reality was to be found in Stamford, I cannot imagine.

We found a condo rental on Maple Avenue, just east of downtown in the Glenbrook neighborhood, and shared it with three other people, a mixed bag of strangers found in the classifieds. This was a period in Connecticut history when the drinking age was eighteen, so I was able to get a cocktail waitress job at the Blue Note, which was only a block from where we lived. Waitressing was the default job of female college dropouts, although I'm not sure what I thought I could do with an art history degree had I completed it. My plan, if it could be called that, was to waitress at night and create art during the day. Skidmore had done that much, instilling in me a sense that women had as much right to a creative life as men. Thanks to Aunt Ginny who taught me how to crochet from a hot pants kit, I was clever with yarn in a time when fiber sculptures were a rising art form. In the 70s, female artists were incorporating traditional domestic skills, such as needlework, into mainstream art (à la Judy Chicago's *Dinner Party*), but it was a concept that soon lost traction. As did I. My shift at the Blue Note started at four p.m. and often didn't get out until two a.m. I slept most of the day.

Like most bars, the Blue Note was hermetically sealed against the cleansing elements of air and sunshine, but it was early in my shift when Joe appeared, so the sun was still up, though sinking fast. The door opened and a flash of slanting yellow light announced his entrance, then it was quickly snuffed out in smoke and darkness as it closed behind him. Joe was alone, chuckling to himself and smiling. The clientele, local ex-jocks from Stamford High, looked up briefly from their beers. If it was rare to have someone of color enter the bar, it was even rarer to have anyone arrive smiling. The crowd was still in a dour frame of mind, not having shaken the day off yet, not having drunk enough to enjoy a short-lived moment of high spirits before the collective mood melted into belligerence or tears—or both. This was the 70s. Lack of money across the board, high unemployment, gas lines, and wild inflation kept everyone feeling shaky. What the fuck was there to laugh about?

I would not call the Blue Note a redneck bar. From what I saw, the regulars welcomed the few black men who wandered in, hoping they'd have some drugs. They usually did, mostly because white folks were always waving money in their faces, begging for pot, smack, or pills. The unemployment rate for black men in the mid-70s was more than 15 percent, spiking in some areas to 30. Wages were low. Drugs were easy money. Often, they were the only money. Joe, however, had not walked into the Blue Note to sell drugs but to sell himself. He liked to go to places that were almost entirely white to find racists and turn them around. He wanted to get under everyone's skin. He believed that as soon as he laid on the charm and intelligence, with which he was doubly blessed, they would respect him and grudgingly become converts to racial equality. He was going to change America one barstool at a time. That was his mission.

A table of women, all white, waved from a far corner. "Joe, come sit over here!" one of them called. He nodded, and the crowd went back to the business of drinking, and I went back to serving them drinks. I was not one of those cocktail waitresses who wore revealing clothes for better tips; it was not that sort of place. I wore a Mexican peasant shirt, with jeans and clogs, and it was all business, even if I was braless. But we were all braless then, it was our claim to freedom, not thinking that it would be more for men's benefit than our own, although I was so flat-chested, there was nothing to gawk at. I forgot about Joe until he leaned back in his chair to block my way. If I'd been carrying anything on my little cork-lined tray it would have spilled, so I shot him a testy look. He looked to be in his midtwenties, tall, but not towering, dark-skinned, with a medium Afro. He was high cheek-boned handsome in spite of a scar that ran down the side of his face like a *mensur,* a fencing cut of honor, as seen on German officers in World War II movies. He was dressed in khakis, loafers, and a white-collared shirt. In a room of jeans and flannel shirts, he stood out not so much for the color of his skin but because he looked like a preppie.

"What's happening, sugar?" he asked. The cumulative cigarette smoke from the table drifted around his head like an apparition.

Oh please, I thought to myself. Nothing was happening at the Blue Note, nothing but me and a hundred drinks to deliver before my night was done.

"What can I get you?" I asked. He stared at me without speaking. His eyelids were naturally heavy, and he made them seem more so by lowering his lashes. He must have believed that his gaze produced an extraordinary effect, and it was not completely lost on me. But I had a boyfriend, and even though Jimmy was four hours away at college, I put up a fire wall. "Well?" I said, maybe a tad sharper than I had intended, with one hand on my hip. This cracked Joe up for some reason, and he laughed so hard he let his head drop and hit the table. I looked at the women, but they didn't seem to know what he found so funny either.

"A mug and a shot of tequila," he said at last, wiping his eyes. He smiled. He had a gorgeous smile, and through the fog of tobacco smoke in the room,

I caught a drift of cologne. Aramis, I found out later, that vintage 60s medley of patchouli and cow leather.

"And another pitcher," said the woman next to him. "We went to high school together," she added, pointing at him, as if I needed an explanation for why he was there.

"Stamford High," said another. "Class of 1968." She shook her head, as if she were counting the years.

It was always standing room only at the bar, and no one ever stood still. I had to elbow my way through a human maze to the service station, shout my order into the bartender's ear, then weave my way back without spilling the shot or losing my grip on the ribbed pitcher. As I leaned in close to Joe to set down the shot and a salt shaker, the tassel on my Mexican shirt swung free over the table.

"$6.50," I said, interrupting him. He was telling the women about a Stamford cop who had been found passed out in his car that day with a mask over his face. The officer had been inhaling crystal meth on duty. He had an Italian name, and Joe seemed to know him. Maybe not personally, but he knew him. The women scoffed.

"Why wasn't it in the paper then, Joe?" one asked, as she crushed her cigarette out on the floor with the toe of her platformed sandal.

"There are more things in heaven and earth, Horatio." Joe turned away from them and gave me a ten, and I was thinking, Horatio? "You keep it, sugar," he said, and I tucked the bill in my glass. The money at the Blue Note was not bad, even for a dive. Sometimes the tips were in drugs: a couple of Black Beauties or a joint. I didn't do drugs myself, so I gave them to the bartender, and he watched out for me, serving me before he attended to his crowd at the bar. Joe's flashy tip should have bought a smile, but my focus was already on the large jocks in the corner pounding an empty pitcher on the table. I nodded and left.

"That bitch is mother-fucking cold," Joe said to his harem. They laughed, and while I was still within earshot, he turned his gaze back on me. "And I'm going to marry her."

I looked at him with his gorgeous smile and rolled my eyes in fake disgust. He always knew how to get a rise out of me. It might have all ended there, with a laugh, except I had to keep returning to the table with more pitchers or shots, and each time Joe used it as an opportunity to hit on me. Each attempt failed to get much of a response, until he landed on the one that did.

He mentioned, in the most offhand manner, that he had run for mayor of Stamford while still a student at Columbia University.

"Were you there?" I asked. "During the student takeover?"

"It was revolution in the streets," he said, not actually answering my question. But I didn't hear that then. Much later, when I worked out the math, I realized that Joe had arrived in Morningside Heights in the fall of 1968, not the spring, breathing in the unsettled dust of the student rebellion the previous May. In high school I had written a paper on the takeover, a document that probably read like a manifesto for upending the world, but I knew the basic facts. The student body, having different agendas, had divided itself along racial lines. The black students were protesting a proposed Columbia gym on public land that would have had a separate entrance and facility for the Harlem residents. In other words, a segregated gym. They were also tired of constant ID checks, which the white students, who were protesting the university's connection with a war-related think tank, were not subject to. So, when the takeover of the administrative buildings began, black students took Hamilton Hall, and the white students took the dean's office. The pain of Martin Luther King Jr.'s murder a few weeks before was still raw. It was an explosive time. Officials were cautious. Care was taken that there would be no newspaper photos of a white cop tear-gassing a black student. Hamilton was stormed fairly calmly by all black officers, a lesson that police departments around the country surely noted.

"Now I'm looking into law school," said Joe. "It'll help me in politics."

Politics? Now we were talking. For most of high school, I worked for the grape boycott on behalf of the migrant farm workers, standing in front of the local A&P handing out pamphlets asking shoppers not to buy table grapes. La Huelga. The United Farm Workers wanted more money, yes, but they also wanted dignity, which meant toilets in the fields. Try explaining that to a suburban matron. Try keeping a straight face while doing it. Later, through the UFW, I held signs for George McGovern. In my senior year, a social sciences teacher encouraged me to apply to American University in Washington, D.C., to major in labor relations or political science, but after I was accepted, my parents said D.C. was too dangerous. "What is it that you want to do that you can't do somewhere else?" my mother asked. It was the first time anyone had asked. At my elementary school, St. Thomas, the few girls who thought ahead had only truncated plans to become teachers or stewardesses until they got married, and it was not much different at Pleasantville High.

We were not encouraged to think ahead. The counterculture reinforced this seeming indifference to our fates. *Be here now* was the mantra of the 70s. Planning for the future was so 50s, so square. In my house in particular, where everything depended on my mother's shifting disposition, to make plans was to court disappointment. Plans for saving the world, yes, plans for me, not so much.

"I want to be a congressman,"* I said, a thought that had never occurred to me before, but it was the first political job that came to mind. It was specific and, I hoped, convincing. I'm not even sure where the idea came from, except to say that I knew I wanted to be a part of the cultural change I hoped was on its way. Politics was the 70s consolation prize for the failed 60s dream, on the theory that the system could be changed more effectively from the inside than from hammering at it from the outside. The battle lines had moved to the courts and legislative bodies. It was a court that had decriminalized abortions in 1973, and it was legislation that allowed a woman to get a credit card in her own name in 1974, the year I graduated from high school. Title IX, another legislative victory, had already passed but was not yet enacted. Too late for me. When I arrived in high school, someone talked me into girls' track. The problem was, there was no girls' track. This was 1970, and in those pre–Title IX days, those of us who wanted to run were allowed—after we had submitted a petition to the school board—to practice with the boys. We were also permitted, if there was room on the bus, to go along with them to meets. Once at the meets, we would—or would not—encounter other girls to race against who found room on their boys' bus. Then we would have to find a coach willing to officiate. The sports bra had not even been invented yet. Coach Geddes, who had only ever coached boys' teams, made some vague gestures with his hands and told us to wear tight bras to keep from . . . then couldn't say the word "bouncing."

My mother snorted when I said I wanted to be a congressman, and my father, who worked on Wall Street, said, "Well, you'd have to be a lawyer for that," as in, *that's* not ever going to happen. Then they stood there and waited for me to get real. This was during one of the frequent 70s recessions, and they weren't about to spend money on tuition unless I had a serious plan. College was probably a conversation we should have had in the fall, when I was applying, not after the fact. But parents and guidance counselors

*We had not yet learned to say "congresswoman," there being so few of them at that point.

were not so obsessed with college admissions as they are today, and certainly not for girls.

"Something in art, then, I guess," I said, and we all shrugged. Skidmore, in safe, leafy upstate New York, was also on my acceptance list, and it met with their approval. Back then, art or art history was one of those degrees, like childhood education or English, that was thought to keep women safely occupied until marriage.

At any rate, when Joe said the word "politics," I imagined that, like me, he was envisioning a new world made possible by progressive legislation that would lift the country's disenfranchised and underprivileged into the light of dignity, community, and justice. Before my shift at the Blue Note was over, between politics and Columbia, Joe had lured me into his life with a glimpse of a world that was fully formed in my head, as if he had seen me sitting at the bottom of my aunt's stairwell taking it all in. But the Land of Love & Freedom would always remain one step ahead of me, and like other mythical kingdoms, the closer I got to it, the more it seemed to fade away. Denise and I had not understood that our own futures lay nearer to that of the girlfriends on the sofa, whose participation in this rock-and-roll idyll was to roll the joints, get the beers, applaud (then fuck) the boys. The youth culture was never any different from the older one. Men were the heroes of their own stories, and women were the support team, but I was a long way from seeing that then.

*O*NE OF THE MANY unexamined expectations I had brought to my relationship with Joe was my belief that we were somehow morally superior to same-race couples. Look at us! We were forging a new, unbiased world, one that would smooth out the edges of race itself, a concept that was societal, not biological. Humans might have different skin colors but are not different races.* But I did not grasp the dismal truth of that statement, that we *are* the same under the skin, which is to say, a deeply flawed and conflicted species. A total mess. By the time I called Denise to ask about Margo, I had reconciled myself to that reality and had become skeptical of everyone regardless of gender, sexual orientation, color, or ethnicity, but there was still a part of me that wanted everyone in an interracial relationship to be free of blame and on the right side of history. Even Howie.

So what I did after I hung up the phone with Denise was, first, to consider that it might have been just a coincidence that Howie said those words about killing someone with a bow and arrow and that, a few months later, his decomposing girlfriend was found with an arrow lodged in her heart. Suspicious, yes, but such hearsay at a card game would probably not even be allowed in a court of law had Howie gotten that far. In this scenario, Howie was innocent and Margo's killer was yet to be determined. This was more or less Joe's version, the one where Howie was a victim along with Margo.

Second in my portfolio of possibilities, which I had begun to dutifully record in my Stamford document, was to consider that Margo's death might have been a drug overdose and that Howie decided to realize his fantasy of

*In 1950, UNESCO issued a statement saying that all humans belong to the same species and that "race" is not a biological reality but a myth.

shooting someone with a bow and arrow after the fact. Maybe in a drug-addled state himself, he even believed it was a romantic gesture in the spirit of Cupid, wounding his victim with Love. Leaving his mark.

Three, I was willing to cede that Howie might have done it, with emphasis on the might, but I envisioned an accident. Yes, an accident. It was possible. Howie might have convinced Margo (or they both accepted a dare from a third person) that he could shoot an apple off her head with an arrow, like William Tell, a feudal serf who refused to bow down to the Man. Not to figuratively bow down but to physically bow to the ground when the local nobleman passed by on his horse. The defiant Tell was sentenced to be executed, but the nobleman wanted to play with his prey first. He gave Tell a chance to earn his freedom by shooting an apple off his son's head with a bow and arrow, which he did, to great acclaim. He was set free and became a Swiss folk hero.

Scoot on up to Mexico in the early 1950s. On a drunken dare, the writer William Burroughs shot an apple off his wife's head with a gun, or rather, shot not the apple but her. She died of a gunshot wound to the head. After paying everyone off, he hightailed it to Marrakech for an extended stay. For the rest of his surprisingly long life, he would refer to this as the William Tell incident. Had Burroughs been brought to justice for the death of his wife, it would have been on manslaughter charges, not murder. Death by misadventure. *Imprudencia criminale.*

Putting a new spin on Joe's story, I expanded on this accident scenario. The Stamford police might well have come to the conclusion that Margo's death was a sick accident but decided that manslaughter was too lenient a charge for her black boyfriend. As I carried this thought to its conclusion, I had to then wonder why they didn't just adjust the evidence to get a murder charge, if they were so determined. But maybe they thought that through too. Even if Howie were convicted for first-degree murder, it would have been highly unlikely for him to receive the death penalty in Connecticut, so the sentence would have only been life in prison. What if, to their minds, that was not enough punishment for a black man who killed a white woman? What if?

WELL, WHY NOT JUST ASK JOE? A couple of decades might have loosened the cards he kept so close to his chest. Emboldened as I was with my three theories I called his mother, Georgia, to get his phone number. It was spring of 2000, and I figured he might well be ready to tell me what had gone down with Howie and Margo, although I knew it wasn't going to be easy. Joe believed that truth was a rare commodity to be doled out to the deserving, so I was prepared to go to New York City, where he'd been living since the 1980s, to buy him dinner and a belly full of drinks. If he sensed that I really wanted to know something, I might even have to pay for the information. Even then, there was still no trusting anything he might tell me, but it would be something.

I had kept in touch with Joe off and on over the years. Or more accurately, he'd call to talk. He always loved phoning old girlfriends, a deep thorn in my side when we lived together, a thorn in my husband's side after we were married, but after a while I stopped hearing from him, although Georgia and I stayed in intermittent contact. She had the same birthday as my father, June 20, so I often thought of her on any celebration of his over the years. While I was with Joe, and for many years after that, Georgia lived in Redding, Connecticut. She was still there at the time of my call. The town is not that far away in miles from Stamford, just a half hour drive northeast or so, but might as well have been a world away, with its quiet wealth modestly tucked away behind unassuming homes. Georgia had lived there since the late 60s, when Cal, a Cadillac salesman, who was older and white, had lured her away from her singing career so they could fight all the time.

Georgia. It was a cliché in those days to say that white girls were searching for the warmth and support that they did not get from their own mothers in the bosoms of black women. What was true and not a cliché was that a white girl couldn't have any interaction with a member of another race, male or female, without someone, somewhere, postulating why. I loved Georgia for herself.

I had heard from Denise, who heard it from friends of friends, that Cal had recently died. In the early 90s Georgia had begun a new singing career in a traditional gospel group, doing some recording and performances, and was giving private lessons, teaching white folk how to sing soul. She was in a good headspace. She had many friends who loved her, so I was sure she'd be fine without Cal. But when I finally reached her, I was surprised that her voice sounded so ravaged.

"I'm sorry about Cal," I said.

"That old man's not dead," she said. "He had heart surgery, so he's living over in Westchester with his 'friend.'"

"Funny," I said. "I wonder where Denise heard that rumor?"

She was quiet. I could hear her light a cigarette and blow out the match. "I'm so sorry I didn't call." She always talked slowly, like the singer she was, enunciating every syllable, paying attention to the sounds. "I lost your number."

In the following silence, I tried to wrap my mind around why she would be sorry that she hadn't been able to tell me about Cal. Why would I care?

"Joseph died a few months ago," she said, in a hoarse whisper. "Cirrhosis of the liver."

"Oh, Georgia."

Oh, Joe. In ancient times, it was the liver, not the heart, that was thought to be the source of human emotion and spirit, and Joe had finally succeeded in killing his. He wasn't even fifty.

And oh, me. I'd had more than twenty years to find out about Howie and Margo, then the moment I'd finally gathered the courage to ask, Joe slipped out of my grasp like water. He had still been very much alive when I called Denise.

"I hadn't seen him for a long time before he came here at Christmas," Georgia said, her voice getting strong with anger. "He was wearing a big baggy shirt. He was trying to hide it from me, but I knew. His stomach was puffed up like a dead cow in a hot field." I heard her inhale smoke. "I knew what that meant. I hounded him and hounded him until he saw a doctor. He was admitted to Mother Cabrini's in January and never left. He died in February."

––––––––––––

ONE STORY I HEARD Joe tell over the years might be completely apocryphal, but it seemed to hold a great deal of meaning for him. It was a story that exposed a deep internal pain and at the same time covered it over with a laugh. Joe never met his father, for whom he was named. The only picture I have ever seen of this man shows him in a navy uniform, probably from World War II. After his service to his country, Joseph Sr. returned home to Bellamy, Alabama, a flyspeck of a town practically in Mississippi, in what is often called the Black Belt of the South. The GI Bill, which had afforded a generation of vets a chance at education and home ownership, as it had for my father when he returned from Korea, was not such a golden ladder for men and women of color. Getting an affordable mortgage meant nothing if no one would sell you a house, as in the same way, education was only free if colleges were willing to open the door, and most often, for black people, they did not. So Joe Louis Sr. picked up where he left off, working in the lumber mill, and in a few years he married the young Georgia Branch of Demopolis up the road, the eleventh of eleven children. Demopolis is under an hour's drive from Selma and just south of Greensboro. When travel writer Paul Theroux visited the town in 2014, he saw worse poverty than he'd seen in Africa or any third-world country he'd ever been to.* Georgia was still in high school when she became pregnant, which is when the heavy-drinking Joseph Sr. began to beat her. Georgia would have none of it, and ten older brothers had her back. After she gave birth to what would be her only child, Joseph Wesley Louis, on November 22, 1950, she swept that baby up into her arms and joined the ongoing mass migration of black Americans out of the South. She moved to Stamford to be near Sam, one of her brothers, and his oversized wife. Joe's uncle was smart, loving, and funny. And he was a janitor. This never kept Joe from thinking big. After all, he watched his dirt-poor mother rise from being a nurse's aide at St. Joseph's Hospital in Stamford to touring the country as gospel backup for B. B. King and Patti LaBelle. As a child, he watched her on *TV Gospel Time*, her own television show.

When Joe was in his late teens, he returned to Bellamy to track his father down, only to find out he'd been hit by a car while walking drunk in the street the week before, then died of pneumonia in the hospital. Joe loved telling people that story, ending it with "that's karma, baby," and having a good laugh at his own expense. He was probably laughing now, at me, that I had missed him by a few months. Everything he knew or suspected about the deaths of Howie and Margo got buried with him in the grave. He died at the same hospital where I was born.

Well, what else can you do but laugh?

*Paul Theroux, *Deep South* (Boston: Houghton Mifflin, 2015).

HEN I WENT to visit Georgia, not long after our phone call, I was surprised to discover two things: (1) Joe had a grown son living in London, of whom more later, and (2) when Joe died, he left behind an unpublished novel called "Hell at the Apostle's Gate." Georgia found the manuscript when she was cleaning out his Tompkins Square apartment in Manhattan after his death. He'd written it in the 90s on an early Mac. It was unedited, and despite its considerable length, possibly unfinished, since it ended with the words "To Be Continued . . . ." Georgia never read it, but her longtime friend, music collaborator, and housemate, Pierre, who grew up not far from her in Redding, did.

"Pierre said not to," she said. "He said it's more than a mother should know about her son." She lowered her voice. "I think he means it's all sex."

I sat at her dining room table, flipping through the pages, trying to catch the words as they flew by. In a 1998 submission cover letter he wrote to Columbia University Press, he said that it was written in the form of a novel for a more enjoyable read, but "it is nonfiction and factually based." The protagonist was Joe Louis and the plot was his life, recounted in the third person from his youth to the time of its writing. It was a life of conquests, sexual and otherwise, a life that had included me. A life that included Margo and Howie.

"Can I get a copy of this?" I asked. It was not seemly asking for favors during a condolence call, but Joe had never stood on ceremony, so in this matter, neither would I.

"Of course, sugar," she said. "That's only the half of it." She got up and rummaged through a box and pulled out some floppy disks. My heart went pit-a-pat. I thought I was going to have all my Howie and Margo questions answered in Joe's own words. He would tell me more dead than he ever would alive. I couldn't wait. I took the disks and the manuscript home and spent a long weekend reading about drugs taken, women slept with, cars driven, political races run, even a meeting with the Black Panthers in New Haven, but no, there were no answers to my questions. It wasn't even a very good read. The narrator was sort of a stiff. At one point, I sent a copy of the novel to Susan Mingus, widow of jazz musician Charles Mingus, whom Joe lived with in the early 80s. Susan's reaction was much like mine. "My overall feeling was that I must have invented the Joseph* I knew—or at least invented him better than he invented himself, or his surrogate. The person in those pages was astonishingly foreign, flat, and not very sympathetic, quite unlike what I found compelling and winning and vital about Joseph himself." The Joe Louis in the novel was the man I knew, but without the wit. Joe was terrifically funny, but for some reason none of that made it to the page. He was too cool, too erudite. He was posing.

But I wasn't looking for Joe, I was looking for Margo. But in the same way that I had left out Margo's death the first time I put the words on paper, Joe had left it out as well. He jumped right over her in the shallow grave, as I had. It was that horrific, that close to home. Maybe, just maybe, if we ignored the dead body, it would simply go away. But why? What were we so afraid of? I would eventually locate the probable source of Joe's fears, of which I knew nothing at the time. As for mine, they became clearer the more I worked on the project. At first, I was ashamed to think my fear was that if it was true Margo was killed by her black boyfriend, maybe I could have been too. But that wasn't the case. I was never afraid of being hurt or killed by the black man I was with—Joe was actively antiviolence on all fronts—but I always carried the fear of being attacked in some way because I was with him. It took me a while to add to my list of theories that Margo could have been killed by some racist, not the random maniac I had conjured in its place but a far more common threat. We were surrounded by people for whom the color of Joe's skin was so abhorrent, so threatening, that my very proximity to him put me in danger. It was a fear I had to keep suppressed to get through the day. For Joe and Howie, that fear was their American birthright.

Joe wrote a single scene with Margo. It takes place at a party at his house in North Stamford, the last place he lived before he met me, and he often spoke wistfully about it. It was a modern home with a pool in an affluent

*Susan and Georgia always called Joe "Joseph."

neighborhood (read: white neighborhood). It was owned by the parents of a friend of his from Cherry Lawn, where Joe had been prepped for college, and the house was sold out from under him late in the summer of 1975.

Bill Borsey, who had a stage name of Willie Deville,* was there with his wife, Toots, who was short, bald-headed, with lots of jewelry and very strange. She claimed to be a witch. Howie showed up with his new girlfriend, Margo, who was the weirdest person that Joe had ever met. She had taken one too many acid trips. She was totally spaced-out and practiced witchcraft and magic. She made Joe nervous.

"This is a nice place you have, man," said Margo, as she gazed all around with a mesmerized look on her face. "I really dig all of the mirrors. It's really trippy."

"Yeah, it seems like a great place to shoot a movie," Willie said.

"They did," remarked Joe. "The movie 'The Swimmer' with Burt Lancaster was shot here. Part of it anyway."

Toots's eyes fixated on one of Margo's necklaces. "I notice that the hexagram you're wearing is tilted on its side. Does that have special significance?" Toots asked Margo, who smiled smugly saying, "Yeah, it does. It symbolizes a special power."

"Are you part of a cult or something? Or do you practice witchcraft or something like that?"

"Well I wouldn't call myself a witch, but I'm into some heavy shit. There's a family I have ties to down in Jersey and Pennsylvania, with some people on the West Coast, but I wouldn't call it a cult or anything. We're all real close, and we know how to make things happen, and keep negative energies from us," Margo said, as she began to perspire heavily. "Yeah, I'm into magic. I really dig mystical things."

"Margo's shit is really out there man. I don't know," said Howie, who laughed as Margo gave him a dirty look.

Margo was not as wobbly-headed as Joe made her sound, although if this account is factual, it seems likely she was tripping when they met. I suspect that Joe was trying to emphasize her cultish inclinations, creating a cover or a reason, perhaps, for what would eventually happen to her, an event that never made it onto the page. It is a scene in which he seems to be casting

*Borsey would soon leave Stamford to form the punk band Mink Deville.

31

around for why this woman would be murdered in under a year. But a fascination with the occult could have been attributed to many of us back then. Margo, along with millions of others in the 60s, was a devoted fan of Carlos Castaneda's bestseller *The Teachings of Don Juan*, which popularized shamanism and mysticism in America. She loved that the lines on the palm of her hand formed a pentagram, a symbol of faith for many Wiccans. I can't imagine why in the novel the hexagram she wears around her neck is tilted, which, if anything, is a Masonic symbol, but Margo might have intended it as the traditional pagan symbol of the union of two opposites, the physical and spiritual, the male and female, the goddess and the god. The Old Religion worshipped nature in a world where men and women were equals, if not matrilineal, and we all dabbled, reclaiming what we believed to be our rightful heritage. We read the *Book of Tao* and threw the *I Ching* for answers to our lives, seeking lost or hidden cosmic powers appropriated from Eastern religions. Joe did too. After a few drinks, he often flattered himself that he was a warlock.

As far as "the family" she says she has ties to, if she said it, she was probably just referring to close friends she made while at Fairleigh Dickinson in New Jersey. Not a cult, as she insists, just a family of her own choosing, a group of like-minded souls discovering their power, using it to repel negative energy. Margo was a caretaker, not a destroyer. When she went to Woodstock* in 1969, she returned with stray cats she rescued at the concert and tried to find homes for them.

Neither Howie nor Joe made it to Woodstock. I tried. Oh, how I tried. I was twelve and staying with Denise at our grandfather's house in Callicoon, ten miles from the concert in Bethel, N.Y. We started to walk there, but our grandfather picked us up outside of town and brought us back. Margo was a lively traveler herself, often hitting the road in her yellow VW bug, taking off for Florida or Arizona, and once hopped a plane to Ireland on a whim. She wanted to see the world, she wanted adventure. She was fearless and perhaps too trusting. After graduating from Fairleigh Dickinson, Margo returned to Connecticut, but not to Darien. Her mother had already moved to Wilton with her stepfather, and her sisters were in college. Margo soon found her people in Stamford, the 60s holdouts who still dropped acid and smoked pot, and one of those people was Howie, the Sky King, the go-to man for

*Featured Woodstock names Richie Havens and Blood, Sweat & Tears played at Margo's high school earlier in 1969.

hallucinogens. He was deeply entrenched in the scene. Their attraction to one another was immediate, and they were living together by the summer of 1975.

For every man who climbs a mountain, there's a woman who sleeps with a man her parents would not approve of. Margo and I had that in common. We set out for adventure in order to find ourselves, and we set out alone with a minimum of survival tools. We left base camp not by climbing out of it but by walking into forbidden arms. Joe would prove to be a challenge not quite on the scale of Everest, but we had our existential moments. For Margo, Howie turned out to be not so much a challenge as a free fall. Conscious or unconscious forces drew her to a man who, by the time I met him, was downright creepy. Her attraction to him might have been just that, the creepiness. The threat. The type of danger that can sometimes feel like love.

It would be interesting to know how Margo's family felt about Howie. She was not living at home at the time she met him, so they couldn't kick her out of the house. But there must have been some strong reactions from this Darien family. I'd heard that Margo's grandfather had visited from Kentucky and taken Howie and Margo out to lunch. The grandfather was politely horrified and tried to get help for Margo through a local UU minister. So, if he met Howie, I'm guessing other family members did too. That's my guess, but there is no one to ask. Margo and I were never alone together to compare our common experiences, and her family has preferred not to talk. I understand. To survive and move on with their own lives, to feel safe themselves, Margo had to be whited out.

If she had any plans to use her childhood education degree in Stamford and become a teacher, she did not seem to act on them. Early on, she worked a few waitress shifts at a delicatessen, but she had her own work as well. She made jewelry and drip candles that smelled of patchouli, selling them to Bear Trader, a head shop in Stamford. So, creatively speaking, she was doing far better than I was.

The first time I met her was in the fall of 1975. Joe and I went to the apartment she shared with Howie. I can't even remember what neighborhood they lived in at the time. It was as if I arrived blindfolded. It was daytime, but the place was dark, lit only by a few slowly sinking candles. The air was heavy with pot, tobacco, and incense, just like my aunt's basement in the 60s, but the smell no longer evoked the Land of Love & Freedom. It was more like the Land That Time Forgot. Margo seemed strange and mistrustful, but she might have said the same of me. I certainly wasn't very forthcoming. Joe and I stood in their living room, which had no furniture, only mismatched sofa cushions and a large, low coffee table covered in wax, ashtrays, rolling papers and bongs. Margo did not enter the room. She leaned against the doorjamb of their bedroom, holding open the Indian bedspread that served as a door. Her eyes on me were hard and appraising. I did not attempt to strike up small talk and neither did she. After a minute, she backed up into her room and let the curtain fall. There was no point in getting cozy with the girlfriends of Joe's friends because they'd be there one day and then disappear the next.

LIKE THE 60S, Margo's murder seemed to fade away the more I searched for it. I had called Denise, I had read Joe's autobiographical novel, but my Stamford story was still going nowhere. It was time to contact the Stamford Police Department to find out whether anyone had ever been arrested for her murder. I had hesitated because I was not predisposed to believe what they had to say. I did, after all, have my story in my pocket, that the police had unjustly killed Howie for Margo's death, and that, if he had pulled back on the bow—*if*—it was probably an accident. When I called the officer in charge of the police archives to enquire about Margo's case, he looked it up while I stayed on the line.

"It's still open," he said, seeming quite surprised. "That's strange."

"Open?" The story of Margo's file would become as mysterious as that of her death. The officer explained that because the case was still open—meaning it was still technically under investigation, unsolved, more than twenty-five years later—he could give me no information. None. Old cases are usually closed in ways called "administrative" or "by other means," such as when the prime suspect dies—that is, by something other than an arrest and conviction. What I didn't know at the time was that no one had opened the file since the day Howie died. Even if they had gathered enough evidence to charge him with Margo's murder, it was a moot point now, and they had gathered no more. You can't convict the dead. It was an ice-cold case and no one but me had any interest in it. Certainly not the police. If I had any journalism training I could have filed a Freedom of Information Act request, but my experience was limited to home-style articles for the *Boston Globe* and various shelter magazines. I'd never needed to use the FOIA to get information on an architect or the Latin name of a shrub. Besides, with the case closed and me a complete unknown to the police, filing a request might not have gotten me anywhere anyway.

"None?" I asked. "You can't give me any information?"

"Sorry," he said, and then he said goodbye.

I called the Stamford district attorney's office, but I was told that the Stamford office opened in 1981 so there were no records from the 70s. Bridgeport would have handled the case if anyone did at all. They didn't. The man I talked to reiterated that no one could talk about the case until it was closed. He laughed. "Keeping the case open is a good way to keep it sealed."

Of course the police would keep Margo's file open and inaccessible. All signs must have pointed to an accidental death, which was unsatisfactory to the police, or perhaps the clues to the real killer were in the file but the police hadn't wanted that person. They wanted the black boyfriend, and they wanted him dead. It fit right into Joe's version of the story, the one where Howie was an innocent man.

*J*HAD BEEN INTRODUCED, if that is the word, to Howie weeks before I met Margo. It was a late September evening that felt more like summer than fall, all hot and muggy even as the sun was setting. Joe and I were at a block party in Stamford's South End, on the other side of the tracks and I-95. Joe owned a gently used blue BMW 2002tii at the time, which he had recently bought on credit. An amazing feat considering he had no credit. But he knew a loan officer at a local bank, a childhood friend of his who slammed heroin on the weekends, the first time I'd heard of junk being recreational and not a full-time occupation. This friend had been the driver in the accident in which Joe acquired the dramatic scar down the side of his face, so this man either approved the loan because he knew the insurance company was going to settle with Joe or out of guilt for disfiguring his face or both. So, with no job and no money, Joe had a late model BMW. I didn't know he was unemployed when we met. He had neatly sidestepped his present situation in our discussion of past glories. When I did find out, I assumed it was a temporary situation, as it was with so many in the recession-riddled 70s, but joblessness turned out to be his philosophical core. In Joe's eyes, any work for a white boss—whether office, day labor, or flipping burgers—meant not just selling out but turning back the progressive hands of history. Joe was at odds with the world. The white world. He would not do it the Man's way. I never argued his point because we both had that innate rebelliousness in us. But because there were few minority-owned businesses in those days, it also meant a severe narrowing of choices. And because he had no job, he had no place to live. He'd been sleeping on couches since he left the house in North Stamford. After we met, he slept mostly in my bed, and even then, I was slow to understand that he did not actually have a place of his own.

But he had this BMW. We drove at parade speed down the street, which was not legally closed even though it was filled with large groups of people—all black and all ages from babies to grandmas, teenagers to moms and dads—and everyone had to move out of the way for Joe's fancy German car and white girlfriend. It was dusk, the air was loud with voices and music. Marvin Gaye's "What's Going On" flowed from a turntable that sat on a windowsill. A band was setting up equipment, running speaker wires around buildings and snaking them through open doors. Oil-drum grills were set up on the sidewalk, producing sweet and smoky smells, and metal garbage cans were filled with ice, soda, and beer. Older folks sat on folding aluminum chairs, the middle-aged perched on curbs, young bloods milled around, and children ran amok, which must have made the presence of a car not just annoying but a hazard. People glared and Joe ate it up. Looking at their faces, I understood for the first time that other people might not like me because of external factors, like the color of my skin, without ever having met me. The black community as a whole had as little tolerance for interracial couples as whites did, worried that it indicated a lack of racial pride in their young people. Many, for good reason, did not trust white people and simply did not like them. I always assumed that I was the object of their scorn that night, but on reflection, it was Joe they barely tolerated. He was slumming, which could not have been lost on any of them. That *I* might have been slumming was completely lost on me.

Joe waved without smiling to a few people, and they reluctantly returned the favor. Out of this crowd walked Howie, and Joe stopped the car in the middle of the street to talk to him. Howie rested both arms on the open window on Joe's side and leaned in to have a look at me. My first impression was that he was tall. Later, I met him when he wasn't wearing platform shoes, and he was medium height. He was thin, with a large puffy Afro and a polyester shirt open halfway down his brown chest, the better to exhibit his medallions. On his fingers he wore silver rings the size of plumbing fittings. In the same way that Margo resembled Janis Joplin, Howie looked like Jimi Hendrix, but he exhaled his words in a Barry White sort of way, only more annoyingly so.

"Where'd you get the pretty pink thing from, bro?" he asked Joe, while staring at me.

"JoeAnn," Joe said, by way of introduction, without looking at me or taking his eyes off Howie. Joe was often reserved, even self-protective, in his interaction with his black friends in a way that he was not with his white friends, a semiotic dance of cool that served to respect space and face. After they exchanged a few gnomic comments on the scene—"Check it out. . . ." "Heavy duty. . . ." "It's out there. . . ."—they performed a simple two-step soul shake, and Joe drove slowly off though the crowd.

I looked at Joe, waiting for an explanation, or at least a name, which was all I got. "Howie Zowie," he said. "The Street Doc-tah."

"Hmmm," I said. Pretty pink thing, my ass. That's all I knew about Howie at the time and all, I felt, I needed to know. A creep is a creep no matter the color of the skin, but what did I care? He and Joe seemed mere acquaintances.

AT SOME POINT early in my mission, I had written Howie's parents asking whether they'd like to talk, but they declined. His mother, Velma, sent me a note saying they did not wish to relive that era, but good luck with my essay. Later, when I returned to Stamford, I could not resist a peek at their house and did a quick drive-by on Shadow Ridge Road, near the Merritt Parkway. The Carter's was a two-story ranch with a neat, square yard and a maroon Buick in the driveway. The homes in the neighborhood were not identical, but they were similar, obviously built at the same time in the early 60s, separated by fenceless lawns at set intervals, as if by a ruler. Except for a few mature trees, landscaping seemed sparse, but it was a happy place, alive with children and minivans at the curb, warming up to go to soccer practice. The neighbors I could see were white. I wondered who had been brave enough to sell Howie's family the house back in the late 60s.

Howie grew up with both parents in the home, and they both worked outside it, which had always been the norm in black families and not part of the seismic change of second-wave feminism that sent white women into the workforce in the 70s. His father worked for the post office, and Velma was a nurse's aide at the local hospital, sometimes alongside Georgia. With two jobs, Howie's family was able to move up the economic ladder and buy the house, but not until Howie was out of high school. His childhood was spent in the Connecticut Avenue projects of Stamford's West Side with two younger sisters. Howie and Joe did not know one another when they were young. Howie was three years older and they went to different schools. In 1965, Howie graduated from the now defunct, but at the time brand new, Rippowam High School up on High Ridge Road. Afterward, he went to Norwalk Community College, but like Joe at Columbia, he must have found the education inadequate, at best. There was nothing a white institution could teach either of them about getting by, so even though Howie was putting himself at a high draft risk, he was out of college at the end of his first year. His family couldn't have been happy. Soon enough, though, they must have been thrilled when Howie passed the civil service exam and got a job at the post office with his father. What could be better than the security and benefits of a civil servant? Especially in Stamford, where civil service seemed like a private club, where, in 1959, the postmaster had been appointed to the position of police chief with no police experience whatsoever. None. Kinsella was still the chief when I lived there.

Howie gave the P.O. his best shot, but he didn't last. In spite of having the role model of his father right there at work, he might not have cared for the way homeowners locked the doors as he approached with the mail or chose another counter to buy stamps. Worse, he would have had to watch his father endure the same treatment. Either way, the 60s must have looked like too much fun to waste it delivering mail, and by 1967 he had stepped off capitalism's middle-class path to become a flower child. He even fell in with some Jesus freaks for a while, and Joe was still teasing him about that years later. Howie was searching, game to try anything that would transform the hard world into something soft and glorious. He sold Owsley LSD before he dealt weed or harder drugs. Acid must have looked like a shortcut to the answers to the big questions. It must have been a good time once, it must have been mind-expanding while it lasted. I had done acid myself at Skidmore and later, when I lived in Boulder. It was fun, but only once in a great while. The first few times you take the acid, after that, it takes you.

Howie and Joe wouldn't meet until the summer of 1968, when Joe was out of high school but before he entered college.

One of Larry's friends, Howie Carter, stopped by with Larry's younger brother, Danny. Howie, who was black, was the quintessential hippie freak. He was really into psychedelia, a real "merry-prankster." He was on acid and on his way to San Francisco by way of his thumb. He was going to leave the next morning.

"So Howie, man, you ever been to Frisco? You're going to hitchhike?" Joe asked.

"No problem, man. If you have the right vibes, you hook up with the right people, and it's one smooth glide. That is, unless you hit a bummer," Howie said and began to cackle.

> Looking at Howie, Joe knew he was one crazy dude, but Joe admired his courage and sense of adventure or sheer foolhardiness.

In Joe's novel there was a lot of vintage Howie, always laughing and slightly maniacal. But by the time I met him, he had morphed from fun-loving to dour and cranky. He seemed to have a lot on his mind and appeared incapable of humor. I never saw him smile, unlike Joe who always smiled unless he had to put on a public face of cool. At best, Howie looked as if he couldn't be bothered. I never witnessed any of the craziness that Joe always attributed to him, which, in those early Richard Pryor days, was not such a bad thing in the black community. In the homes of friends who owned turntables, we'd listen to Pryor's *Bicentennial Nigger*, "celebrating 200 years of white folks kicking ass." To say "that nigger's crazy" (the title of another Pryor album) was half a compliment, something to be admired, because it implied a certain recklessness in the face of white hate and power. Insanity was a sane response to an insane world.

Everyone was co-opting the language of their oppressors, hoping to drain it of its power. Women called each other bitch. Joe and his black friends called each other the N-word. Georgia used that word when she was angry with him.

But the N-word was no laughing matter. Its power never drained. We went to Boston every few months to visit John and Sylvie Young, another interracial couple, originally from Stamford. They lived on Mission Hill in Roxbury, and John woke up at 4 a.m. every day to bake bagels for a living, but his real life lay elsewhere—in Sylvie, in his friends, and lessons in African tribal dancing. School desegregation was not going well in Boston in 1975. Racial tension over busing was high. Sometimes I think we were nuts to be visiting Boston as often as we did. Sometimes I think that that's exactly why we went. Joe claimed that he'd rather do battle with a real racist than tolerate the false niceness of a hypocrite. He was pretty innocent that way, and lucky. An interracial couple was the physical manifestation of everyone's worst fears, and we were an open target for white anger. Sylvie told me that one night, walking along the street with John, a group of white teenagers began to stalk them, shouting out "nigger lover." She begged John not to respond, and even though John looked like he could crush anyone between two of his fingers like a peanut, he didn't. The important thing was to get Sylvie, four months pregnant, home without incident. But when they got there, she lost the pregnancy anyway in a spontaneous miscarriage. She blamed it on the scene in the street and wondered whether she'd ever have a baby, since there would always be those scenes. She did eventually carry a baby to term, but the last I heard she'd had a breakdown and was in an institution.

IN 1969, Howie approached Joe, the younger dude with the smarts and New York connections, about dealing pot together. Joe wrote:

> Howie began to pace the floor, decked out in leather-patched jeans and suede vest with a flowered shirt and a diamond stud in his ear. "Look man," he said to Joe, "I'm not you. I don't want to be a doctor and a politician, the president or some shit. I just want to have some cash, a lot of nice chicks, a hell of a lot of good drugs, and a place to do them in."

That was Howie's mission. Joe was on full scholarship, including room and board, but he needed spending cash. He was not one of those scholarship students willing to do any job the university proposed. He would not bus tables in the school cafeteria because that meant cleaning up after white students. So, when Howie suggested an alternative, Joe was ready.

They raised money to purchase inventory wholesale in New York City, and Joe began to bring bricks of weed back to Stamford on the weekends. He and Howie rented a house together on Wolf Pit Avenue in nearby Norwalk, and Howie ran the retail operation, baggie by baggie. This arrangement lasted for almost two years, a long time in the trade and a reflection of their business acumen. But smarts and luck don't last forever. Their house was raided, and they were busted for possession of hash early in 1971, which amazingly did not result in jail time for either of them. Howie wiggled his way out in some way or another, and Joe called civil rights attorney Manny Margolis, who took his case after Joe convinced him he was a political prisoner. The bust put the fear of incarceration in Joe, and at least while I knew him, he never dealt drugs again. The greater fallout was that it linked Joe and Howie together forever in local police files.

*I*N JANUARY 2009, on the day of the inauguration of America's first black president, nine years after Joe had died, I called Georgia to ruminate about Obama, whose parents' interracial marriage was illegal in sixteen states when he was born in 1961. Rush Limbaugh and other white supremacists called him a Halfrican. Donald Trump claimed he wasn't an American at all.

"Who would have thought this would happen in our lifetimes?" I asked, amazed and pleased, although I was still carrying a flame for Hillary, wondering why it had come down to a black man and a white woman in the primary. Why did we have to choose between the two?

"I knew," said Georgia. "Joe knew. He said he was going to be president since he was in the fifth grade."

Joe had entered Stamford's public school system with that all-American, all-white, male dream of being president someday clutched in his little brown hand. It was an exuberant moment, when the years of civil rights activism and sacrifice were finally paying off, at least for some of the country's black children. This was in the days when equality meant assimilating black culture into white, an effort to make the best and brightest "more like us." To a point. Equal education was the word of the day, equal encouragement, not so much. Joe was actively discouraged from this president thing. When he was in the fifth grade, the principal called Georgia into the office to express his annoyance at the very idea and said her son had better come up with a different answer the next time he was asked what he wanted to be when he grew up.* Georgia was livid, not just because he was crushing her

*Malcolm X was one of the top students in Junior High in Lansing, Michigan, and when his teacher asked what he wanted to be, he said a lawyer. His white teacher said why not be something more practical, like a carpenter.

boy's dreams, but because she'd had to take unpaid time from work to hear his racist crap.

She enrolled Joe into the now defunct Stratford Military Academy in New Jersey, an elementary boarding school, where he was the only black student. For high school, he entered all-male and largely white Fairfield Prep in Darien, but it did not last. The priests, who may or may not have been racist, were openly anti-Semitic, and Joe refused to accept that his Jewish friends were not getting into heaven because of it. When Joe pointed out to a priest that Jesus was a Jew, he was asked to leave. No matter. The Jesuits' religious intellectualism did not mesh with the deep spiritualism of the African Methodist Episcopal Church Joe was raised in anyway. His mother, after all, was a prominent gospel singer, so there was nothing they could teach Joe about God. Besides, he didn't cotton to the all-boy classes anyway. He wanted to get his hands on some girls, especially white girls, who, in 1965, were beginning to look at boys like him with curious eyes.

Off he went to Stamford High, where he became part of a large black minority, but he was still special. According to Joe, he was carried around on a velvet pillow and loved every minute of it. The 60s were copacetic, as he would say. He went to afternoon and summer classes at Cherry Lawn Prep in Darien, courtesy of the federal government and the school's trustees, who were getting him ready for the big show, making an Afro-Saxon out of him and sprinkling a little brown sugar on their white student body in the process. Smart as a whip, that one. Everybody wanted a piece of him, as he made clear in his novel.

> One of the most beautiful aspects of the sixties was that whites felt a genuine sense of guilt concerning their historic treatment of blacks. Accordingly, even if one were a racist, one would not want to appear as such. Everybody acted as if they loved "colored people." And in Stamford and places like it, everyone was trying to be more liberal than the next. It was great for Joe, and boy did he play on it. He would never dream of reacting with animosity toward the jocks. Joe would rather smile and give them some flowers, hell maybe even a kiss. He knew he had them working for him. . . . The world was changing at a startling rate and people were scared. They really did not know what was going to happen next. Reis Taylor being with Joe Louis was only a small example of this phenomenon.

When Joe wrote these words in the 90s, the 60s were still a warm glow in his memory, a time when equality and love merged, and dark-skinned Joe Louis was able to openly date the fair Reis. They were together in high school and well into college, and I was never sure how it ended. I just know that she moved to California with her family and never came back. Her parents had been fully accepting of Joe, so it wasn't as if they were whisking her away from him. You could say they embraced him. Joe told me a story about how he and Reis's mom almost kissed, inching closer and closer to each other on the sofa until, just at the critical moment, her husband walked in. This could have been Joe's erotic imagination, or it could have just been the 60s.

Margo and I would not be viewed so fondly by society and our families as Reis had appeared to be. In the 60s, she and Joe were a far-out novelty, romanticized in the Broadway musical *Hair*. In the 70s, interracial couples were looking more like a dangerous trend that had to be derailed.

IN HIS SENIOR YEAR, Joe was offered full rides at a number of Ivy Leagues, including Harvard, but he chose Columbia because of its easy access to Stamford, an hour commuter train ride away. Joe still believed he could live in both worlds, the rarified campus of the white elites and what was left of the historically black neighborhoods of Stamford, but by the time we met in 1975, he no longer felt that way. He believed that one more step into white institutions—meaning, working for the Man, who couldn't buy slaves anymore but loved to rent them cheap—would be a betrayal of his real self, his black identity. And yet, it seemed that dating white women was no betrayal at all.

The one job he actively pursued, that of mayor of Stamford, turned out to be not what I had imagined. On July 1, 1971, the voting age was dropped from twenty-one to eighteen, and on that day Joe registered to vote and announced his candidacy. He was twenty years old. In the fall, he was back at Columbia and came home to campaign on the weekends. After a couple of months, during which much of his election effort was spent trying to keep his recent drug bust with Howie a secret, he failed to get the backing of the local black Democratic caucus. To spite them, he left the race and threw his support to the white Republican, who won. Joe thought he'd be appointed to some plum post in the city government for his trouble. He went to the mayor to discuss what he called in his novel "his piece of the pie." After a curt exchange of words, he was given a meager slice in the corporation counsel's filing room. Considering it an affront to his intelligence, he only lasted a few months at best. It was the one real job he ever had.

Did I know all this about supporting a Republican, the party of Nixon? No, of course not. Not until I read his novel and cross-checked his information with the *Advocate* archives. Georgia had once hinted at it, but I only saw what I wanted to see. Joe ran for mayor and I read everything else into that. He knew exactly what details of his political experience would appeal to me and what to omit.

But at Columbia he was very much not a Republican. Even though Joe missed the campus uprisings of the spring of 1968, he wore blacker than thou politics on his dashiki sleeves, keeping it lively with the brothers and enjoying the street theater of ongoing demands and demonstrations. Between selling pot with Howie and campaigning for mayor, there was not much time for studying. Joe spent four years at Columbia, at first taking care to keep his grades well above water and his carcass safe from the draft. But as time went on, he did not want to be seen putting too much effort into school and pursuing the white man's goals, so he failed to graduate with his class in 1972. He claimed he only had to make up a single course to get his diploma, but it was worth nothing anyway because street smarts were what mattered in this world. Yes, I nodded, yes. I, too, had questioned the value of a diploma over life experience. Of the four of us in 1975—me, Joe, Margo, and Howie—only Margo had actually graduated from college prepared to carve out a future of her own.

What happened to Joe, the kid who was going to be president? He had achieved what the civil rights movement had hoped for him, a golden education with all the connections and opportunities that went along with it, but affirmative action and scholarships could not give him what he really wanted. He was a child of the 60s and he wanted what his white male friends had, and it wasn't just privilege. He wanted the right to reject it too. And so he did, renouncing America and capitalism as loudly as any suburban white boy sleeping on Aunt Ginny's sofa once had. Joe didn't understand that they could afford to. They risked nothing. The door had always been kept open for them, for whom the system had been made. When the economy turned brighter and lucrative jobs became available, they just washed off the patchouli oil and walked back into the game. The rules were not so flexible for minorities and women who had only just been grudgingly allowed to board the bus, and only if there was room.

If Joe had been born a few years later, he might not have been so quick to reject his options. For one thing, Cherry Lawn closed in 1972, so he would have had no prepping. For another, in the tanked economy of the 70s, affirmative action was fueling racism. Quota became a dirty word. It was a zero-sum world, baby, and white bottoms were beginning to miss their velvet pillows. In Joe's novel, he finished his section on the 60s with these words:

> This perception that events and circumstances were transpiring outside of their (white) realm of influence led to a feeling of impotence and deep-seated hostility which would rear its ugly head with a vengeance one day in the not too distant future.

The 70s recoil was on its way.

ANY OF JOE'S former classmates from Stamford High had largely sat on their racism during the 60s, but in the 70s there wasn't as much social pressure to embrace civil rights, so they didn't. Only now they were not in high school anymore, but at the Blue Note, and I was waiting on them.

"This is bullshit," Joe said, standing at the door, not bothering to lower his voice. It was late, and he was about to leave. He usually stopped in at the Blue Note every few nights, but he'd been doing that since before my time, like a friendly neighborhood pup. He had a set round of bars to sniff out, seeing who might buy him a drink, lend him money, or simply gather information that might come in useful down the road. He gestured at the white clientele. "I don't want you waiting on these honkies. They're all just a bunch of drunks."

Had I known him longer, I would have found that remark pretty funny, considering the source. As it was, I just said no. "I have rent to pay," I said, thinking he might see the wisdom in this, considering the condo was the closest thing he had to a place to live as well.

But no. He executed an end run with a kiss. On my lips, in front of everyone. Then he left. I didn't think anything of it. The mechanics of racism were still a mystery to me, but not to him. In 1975 it was dangerous enough to be in an interracial relationship; in a place like the Blue Note it was sheer recklessness to kiss out in the open, which implied both ownership and a whiff of sex. We hadn't been keeping our relationship a secret, but neither were we flaunting it. Joe rarely stayed long, and I was always busy with customers anyway. After our kiss goodbye, as I went back to serving drinks, two guys started outside after him. Someone, I don't know who, tried to stop them, and then all drug and alcohol-fueled hell broke loose. A dozen men were suddenly fighting, men who certainly had no idea what or who they were fighting for or against, but in a crowded area one bump or jostle quickly led to a fist. Joe was long gone. "Make love, not war" was his motto, then run for cover. A chair flew through the air like in a Western, and I was so amazed I just stood and watched. The bartender, who was not much older than I was, lifted me up and dropped me behind the bar until it was over, wondering at my inability to recognize approaching danger.

"You didn't even see that coming, did you?" he asked.

I shook my head. "No." I didn't see the chair coming, and I didn't see that Joe had manipulated the situation. I only saw his righteousness, which he wore on his shoulder like a badge of honor, a badge I coveted. The bartender kindly suggested that this was not the right place for me. He was not some awful bigot—I don't even think he disapproved—but he knew that an interracial couple had the power to empty a room. Which was more than I knew. My understanding of race in America was sorely incomplete.

———————

I WAS SEVEN YEARS OLD when my family moved to Pleasantville as part of the white flight out of the Bronx in the early 60s, and it was nearly an all-white community when I was growing up.* From the constrained vantage point of St. Thomas Elementary, a parish school run by nuns, I watched the 60s truck on by in my plaid school uniform and tight braids. Fed by the visions of the counterculture in my aunt's basement, in the fall of 1970 I entered Pleasantville High School, where I thought my real life was about to begin.

I had not understood that the Kent State killings in May 1970 were the beginning of the 60s twilight in more than just the turn of a decade. That September, the first month into my freshman year, Jimi Hendrix died of a barbiturate overdose. The students at our school held a candlelight vigil, and when Janis Joplin died a couple of weeks later from a heroin overdose, we held another. Throughout the year there were more vigils as students died or became crippled from various ODs and drunk driving accidents, until at last, on July 3, 1971, after the end of my freshman year, one more candle was lit for Jim Morrison, who slipped silently under the suds in a Paris hotel bathtub. The bloom had come off the flower child, and it was no longer

———

*Sidney Poitier and his family lived in town, but his daughters went to my high school after I had graduated.

reasonable to believe I could grow up to be a hippie. The revolutionaries, such as they had been, were gone, or worse, co-opted by the system. A few, like the Weathermen, went underground, embracing pipe bombs and bank robberies to overthrow the government. Others turned their backs on the system altogether and joined the back-to-the-land movement,* relocating to isolated rural areas to live off the grid and milk the goats. It was the 70s, and most everyone felt disenchanted with the world. Even the palette changed with the collective mood, from the bright 60s colors of Day-Glo yellows, pinks, orange to the 70s more natural but often grim shades of faded blues, moody greens, and mauve. I often bemoaned being part of that sorry-ass decade. Somehow, I felt that if I had arrived at the revolution in time, it would not have faltered. But I did what I could. Besides working for the UFW grape boycott, I was the editor of the school paper for a while and changed the name from the *Neperhan* to the *Student Voice*. Within a year, the principal took the job away from me for publishing a photo of students on the high school lawn smoking pot. One of those students was me, but it was staged. I wanted to hang with the kids who smoked pot but didn't care for it myself. I never really took to altering my mind with anything other than books. I took as many literature courses as I could, including an elective called Black Literature, where I read the canon from Frederick Douglass to Malcolm X, the black canon being at the time as male as the white canon. Regardless, it was clear that we, the white race, were a bunch of bullies. When Malcolm wrote about the white devil, that was us. We read *Soul on Ice*. It seems inconceivable to me now that it was part of the syllabus, considering that Eldridge Cleaver had once been a serial rapist of white women as a payback to slavery. He looked back on those acts as reprehensible, but still. The book has not held up well on rereading. It seems a mishmash of racial politics and violent misogyny, rambling psycho-sexual-racial babble.** But who among us would not start babbling in prison, where much of it was written?

I don't remember what I thought of the book then, or whether I was appalled at the sexual violence, but I loved to carry it around with me. We were in thrall to the culture, including the teacher, a young white man who might not have felt empowered to pass judgment on the material. And yet, no one then considered the privilege implied in the fact that white literature was

*Bernie Sanders was one of these.
**Cleaver went from being a Black Panther leader to a conservative, evangelical Republican before he died in 1998.

the core curriculum and black literature the elective. And with no people of color in the student body, it was as if we were studying an ancient civilization with no connection to our lives. Racism was taught as something outside our personal history, not as an institutionalized part of the dominant culture. The very fact of the school's whiteness, of our families having been able to leave the distressed city behind and buy homes in the suburbs and the black families had not, was never addressed.

But at least they offered the class. There was no Women's Lit, so I was on my own with that. I got my hands on a copy of Elizabeth Janeway's *Man's World, Woman's Place*, which examined how recent the cult of female domesticity was, with women assigned to living "around the edges of events." For extra credit, I wrote a paper. My English teacher, a white man, trashed my praise, insisting that the book was all rhetoric and didn't say anything. Janeway, one of the great critical minds of the times, was waved away as fluff. I did not get the extra credit.

At Skidmore, there were few students of color of either gender.* The school, to keep us from getting on the train to New York City every weekend, tried to keep us entertained. Dances were fueled with Stevie Wonder, soul, and R&B. In the same auditorium where I looked at art slides, they showed the 1973 classic flick *The Harder They Come*, and we all fell for reggae. Disco was music to make fun of. It was not "real," it was orchestrated, and yet the words were singed with seduction and fraught with despair, so we were pulled in nonetheless. There was a black bar in Saratoga called the Grill that had a dance floor with a mirrored ball. Thursdays were White Night, when the regular clientele split to leave us college girls to dance the bump with townies and each other to the beat of "Lady Marmalade."

There was no organized grape boycott and sadly, none of the student rallies against the Machine that I had expected from the college experience. Instead of protests, there were petitions. One, in particular, was to free Joan Little, the young black woman in North Carolina who stabbed her white jailer/rapist to death with the ice pick he carried into her cell. When she was acquitted in 1975, it was the first time a court had agreed that a woman had the right to defend herself, even unto death, against sexual assault. The first time.

*Like many of the all-women's colleges at the time, Skidmore had recently gone coed, clocking in at around 10 percent men, mostly dance majors.

Signing petitions felt sorely inadequate. I left Skidmore thinking I could find another way. How did Joe know that when he walked into the Blue Note, I'd be there, waiting for someone just like him? There is certainly a part of me that may have been more interested in being the person who was with Joe than with Joe himself. Still mourning the idealized 60s that I never got to experience (and who, in the end, really did?), being with Joe felt like a political act, and an automatic backstage pass to those days. I would join the 60s generation by osmosis, and Joe's color would envelop me in the spirit of the civil rights movement. My eyes were gazing at the smoldering embers of the golden age. It was not too late to stir the ashes.

And yet, after that first night with Joe at the Blue Note, I did not call home to tell my parents about this neat guy I just met. I certainly didn't call Jimmy. I thought Joe and I would hang out for a while, and through him I would connect with the world of social activism in Stamford, and at some point the relationship would die a natural death. I did not recognize the tremendous privilege buried in that attitude, in thinking I could just try out the black experience, then retreat back into my safe, white world with no one knowing. But no. I fooled around and fell in love, as Elvin Bishop used to say.

A week or so after Joe and I met, Jimmy was due to arrive for a visit. I didn't know what to do, so I did nothing. Joe forced my hand by refusing to leave my apartment. To prevent the two of them from colliding, I broke up with Jimmy by phone. He had been my first real relationship, and while we had drifted apart in the past year, I wished that this painful private moment would not have to take place in such a public space, the hall phone of his dorm. But there was no other option. I was a coward.

"Don't come down this weekend, there's somebody here," I said in a rush, instead of saying the truth, that our relationship was over. I followed this with the rather inane, "I wish you could meet him. You'd like him."

After a brief explosion of words, Jimmy jumped in his car and drove to Stamford. Clearly enjoying this crisis of his own making, Joe abdicated his position with a grin and a wink and left the house, leaving me with an angry ex-boyfriend. On the way out the door, Joe said, "Make sure you take your pill tonight, sugar."

Joe was a dangerous romantic. Or just plain dangerous. In our first week together, he'd thrown my birth control pills out the window of a moving car. "We're leaving our future to fate" was all he said about that. Did I? Give me more credit than that. There were more pills where those came from. Still, I was impressed with his recklessness, even though it was my life he was being reckless with.

When Jimmy arrived, I sent him packing back to his school in upstate New York. Do I sound cruel? I didn't think so. I felt bad, but not wrong. We'd been together for nearly three years, and he still didn't know whether he loved me. As is so often the case, after it was over, he decided he did. A week after his visit, I received a box in the mail with a banner-length computer readout, complete with old-school dot matrix print and cog holes along the edges, saying "I Love You." But it was too late. Joe knew the moment he saw me that he loved me, and he said it often. And I was young and insecure enough to want to see myself reflected in adoring eyes.

If real life was what I was after when I left college, then this, I assumed, was it. Joe seemed to have something that could be borrowed—let's call it soul—that seemed to be lacking in my own life. Maybe I was even expecting black culture to heal me of the American wound of slavery, and from then on, I would be exempt from blame.

––––––––––––––––

THE MAPLE STREET CONDO fell apart within days of my leaving the Blue Note. First, Christie left because someone turned on the heat and melted her record collection, which was leaning against the baseboard heater. It could have been Joe, but more likely it was a housemate who was always complaining of being cold, even though fall had just begun. At any rate, Christie had no great fondness for Joe, not because of his color, but because he was drifting, and she was afraid I'd start drifting along with him. She was right. After she moved to Colorado for another stab at college, I didn't have the money for rent, and besides, Joe didn't want to stay with increasingly hostile housemates. With nowhere to go and no jobs, our lives became a chaotic blur. Joe and I lived on almost no money, most of that borrowed from his mother or from his wide circle of friends, crashing on the floors and sofas of those same people.

We didn't even have a car. Joe's BMW had been totaled before he made a single payment. Not that he had the money for a payment. He slammed into the back of his mother's car late one night as we were following her home to Redding from a bar. Georgia had stopped her car on the dark rural road to get out and yell at a newspaper guy for stopping his truck to deliver bundles. She was just telling him how he could cause an accident in the middle of the road like that, and then we came around the corner and hit the back of her Cadillac. As accidents go, it wasn't a bad one. My head tapped the windshield because I wasn't wearing a seatbelt, but the Beemer's catalytic converter got stove in, which in those days was enough to total it. Joe used the AAA number of an old girlfriend and had it towed away for the bank and insurance company to deal with. Georgia's Cadillac had an imperceptible dent on the bumper.

So, without a car and no public transportation to speak of, it was impossible for either of us to get a job, and without at least one of us employed, we could not get a place to live, even if we could have found an apartment we could afford. Or a landlord who would take us. Being without an address meant no phone, no shower, and no clean clothes for work, which would have gone a long way to getting a car.

But in the end, losing the BMW was just as well. Not only could Joe not afford it, he soon had his license suspended for an old DUI that had been pending in court around that time. I didn't have a car of my own, but I had just gotten my Connecticut license, so when Joe was able to borrow a car here and there, I began to do all the driving. Almost. Interpreting his suspension as being racially motivated, Joe took the wheel every now and again just to show them they couldn't keep him from driving. It turned out they could. One night, when we were cruising through downtown Stamford, Joe got frustrated with what he called my pussy-ass driving—meaning full stops at red lights and going the speed limit. We argued. "Let me drive," he said. Fine. I got out at a light, he got in, we drove one block, and he got stopped by the police.

One block. Oh, the cops, they were always watching.

Joe got taken away in handcuffs. I tried to follow the police car, but they lost me, which Joe later said pleased them no end. When I finally found the station, the officer at the desk lied and told me there was nothing to be done, so I drove all the way back to Pleasantville. I wasn't going to sleep on Joe's friend's sofa without him. Joe was furious that I had left without posting bail. As if I had that sort of cash. He called an old girlfriend to bail him out. I didn't make that mistake again and learned to carry a bondsman's number with me at all times. Alan P. Fishman. I found his card in a wallet stored in a box with some photos from those days. It is one of the rare artifacts that survived, and although I never needed to call on the good graces of Mr. Fishman, Joe and I were stopped many times during the two years we were together, regardless of who was driving. As Joe said, it just "went with the skin."

You are probably thinking, poor dears, of course their life together was a mess, what with racism raining down on the two lovebirds in those unenlightened times. It would be nice to say that the times had changed. It would be nice. But a quick glance at the headlines across the country reaffirms that Driving While Black, or With Black, is still a violation of some unwritten law, and Running While Black can get you shot in the back. And yet, this being Joe Louis, some of our troubles were of our own making. Yes, being harassed by the police went with the skin, but keeping a license, registration, and car in order would have gone a long way to mitigate it. But that would have meant playing into a system that Joe believed was stacked against all people of color.

Then there was Joe's drinking. I had attributed his increasingly frequent mood swings, when darkness would suddenly cover his bright shell, to the daily stress of racism, when what I was really looking at were hangovers. I couldn't see then that the two might go hand in hand. As smart as he was, he felt that no success would ever be considered legitimate. When he went to Columbia, many people thought he got in only because he was black. The reality is, affirmative action encouraged schools to overlook the color of his skin and accept him for his smarts. Yet he knew what his classmates thought, that he was not their equal. He heard the disdain in their voices. It was certainly a factor in preventing him from moving forward with any career, the fear that it would always appear as if he hadn't earned it.

Being the object of constant hate and discrimination surely calls for some sort of self-medication. You have to find a way to zone out. I certainly did. I wrapped myself in a self-protective haze, blind to the dangers of the streets and the hostile glares of disapproval around us. That took energy. I slept a lot. We once went to a loft in Stamford to hear T. S., the son of Thelonious Monk, do some drumming with other musicians. We were standing by the door, looking in, and I was leaning against the doorjamb with my eyes closed, sleeping on my feet like a horse. Joe shook my arm and told me to stand up straight, he didn't want people to think I was a junkie.

Margo and Howie used drugs to zone out, living in the clandestine world of dealing and using, full of secrets and whispers. And yet, they had an apartment, which was more than Joe and I had, so who can judge whose life was more fucked up? All this crashing on sofas reminded me of my aunt's basement, but it no longer had the aura of freedom and rebellion that I had once read into it. If you are sleeping on a different sofa every few nights, something has gone very wrong with your life.

Having said that, it was amazing how many of Joe's friends accepted homelessness as a completely normal state, correctly assuming that I could not fall back on my family—who, except for Denise, were still not aware of Joe's existence—for help. We slept on floors and sofas, not just in Stamford, but at his friends' homes in upstate New York and Boston, and on rare occasions at Georgia's. We sometimes spent our days at Kenny's, a white guy Joe knew from his days at Cherry Lawn. Kenny and his wife, Paula, had a big house in North Stamford, and they had a little girl who once asked why Joe's skin was chocolate and everyone else's vanilla. Her parents thought it was the cutest thing and repeated the anecdote every time we saw them. I'm sure they repeated it to others. It spoke so well of them. It showed that (1) they had a black friend, and (2) they were so open-minded their daughter didn't even know that there were such things as different races. What it really showed was that their daughter had never seen a single other black person up there in North Stamford. I could see that many of Joe's white friends were in it for the glamour of having a black friend, without ever thinking it had anything to do with me.

For all the time we hung out there, we never spent the night. We were never invited, perhaps because they knew we might never leave. At night we'd often go from there to Ronny and Leila's, who lived in St. John's Towers. They were another interracial couple, and they invited us to stay with them as often as needed. They were married and had a tan baby and were thinking about another. Over the years Leila's white mother had taken tiny steps in accepting Ronny, especially since the birth of her grandchild, and had recently taken a big step in having them all to dinner. During the time we stayed with them, the St. John's tenants' rights group had been blasting the cops and the management firm that ran the Towers for lack of security, with vandals, drug addicts, and muggers living in the halls. The police responded to the protests by saying, yes, it was a dangerous place, but they lacked the manpower to do anything about it. And then they shrugged.

But the sofa Joe and I slept on the most was owned by Carol Sullivan, a white woman in her thirties who looked much older and lived on Court Street in Stamford, a sad neighborhood that was and is predominantly black. She lived in a ground floor apartment of a one-family home that had been cheaply converted to multiple units. Like the other houses on the street, it had only a distant memory of paint, a swaybacked porch, and a TV antenna that hung limply off the roof. The street was run down and in disrepute back then and is so bad today that the police have placed Jersey barriers on one end to close off access to Washington Boulevard, a main artery through town. This measure makes drug surveillance easier and insures that no innocent (read: white) visitor to the city enters by accident. To get there, you have to know it exists in the first place. Joe once said that he'd rather be homeless than to have the stigma of a ghetto address like Court Street.

Carol had two pale teenage daughters living with her, and if there had ever been a husband or boyfriend who fathered them, he was long gone. I haven't a clue how Joe and Carol met, but they seemed to have known each other for many years, going back to Joe's childhood. She might have been his babysitter, but for all their long association, she didn't get a single mention in Joe's novel. She had known Howie for a long time too, and then she knew Margo for as long as she lasted. I liked Carol. She was kind to me, and I sorely regret that I could not have been kinder to her later on, when she needed the comfort of a friend.

IN THE MIDDLE OF OCTOBER, I went to my parents for a quick visit on my birthday. I was nineteen feeling like ninety. Joe would turn twenty-five a week later. He was proud of being a Scorpio, which he felt was a far superior sign than my lowly Libra. My mother was a Scorpio too, and she claimed it was the very best sign as well, as if they were rooting for the same sports team. My mother asked how Christie was. "Is she still with that guy she was with this summer?"

"No," I said, a lie on so many levels. I had never told her that Christie was no longer my roommate and had moved to Colorado. I never told her that I was living on the sofas of strangers. I never told her that I had broken up with Jimmy. Christie was, in fact, still seeing that guy my mother was referring to, but I decided I would test the ground. I knew my parents would not be happy about Joe, but I wasn't sure how strong the response would be. Except for one joking remark my father had made while we watched *Guess Who's Coming to Dinner?* on TV one night when I was young, they had never said anything outright racist. But the implicit racism of the culture, and the very fact of our white bubble, made me know that an interracial relationship was totally unacceptable.

"Actually," I continued, with some hesitation, "she's dating a black man."

"What do her parents think about that?" she asked.

"They're perfectly fine with it," I said, following one lie with another.

"Really?"

Really.

I was still trying to have it both ways, be with Joe without having to pay the full price of being with him. I wanted him cheap. I had dropped out of school in search of a more authentic life, yet I couldn't step up to the plate and admit that I was in love with Joe, a black man. I was totally inauthentic.

WHEN OUR FIRST Christmas was upon us, I was living back in Pleasantville. Early in December, I had begun to buckle under the stress of homelessness. I hated being at the mercy of Joe's friends, depending on handouts, not knowing where we'd sleep any given night. With no stability, I could not get even the lowliest waitress job to turn that situation around. The more stressed I became, the more Joe insisted I buck up. This was life, he insisted. It was certainly his life. I was not so sure anymore that I wanted it to be mine. Not when Joe announced he was leaving for Philadelphia to sell his stereo system for $500 to his old girlfriend, Janet. She already had the stereo in her possession but told him he had to go down there to get the money in person, and there was no room for me in that scenario. We fought, and I was out of there. I packed up my things, such as they were, and he drove me to Pleasantville. But when he dropped me off at my parents that night in a Volvo borrowed from an old girlfriend, I got out with an armful of dirty clothes and a hole in my heart. I didn't even say goodbye. My mother said nothing as she held the door open, but she radiated anger. She didn't know about Joe and could not have seen him drop me off, so who knows what that was all about.

I sobbed for days. Days and days. Our house was so large I don't think anyone heard me. If they did, no one came to see what was the matter. I started thinking about state schools, student loans, and scholarships, since I knew my parents would not be willing to pay for a second shot at a private college. They did not ask what I intended to do and did not suggest I go back to school. I had renounced my educational privilege and found it was hard to get back in. Deadlines were months down the road and fall admittance was a lifetime away. I got an ill-paid lunch shift as a hostess at a restaurant a few miles away in White Plains, seating cranky shoppers from Macy's. A week later, Joe called, and I was back. An arrow had pointed to the path away from him and I did not take it, because on the other path was a hostess job that barely paid the transportation costs to get there, an unwelcoming homelife, and the distant possibility of college, for which I was unable to formulate a goal. Life with Joe was chaotic, but it was a life. His life. It had not yet registered that I could have my own.

I did not move out of my parent's house since there was no place to move to, but I started to spend occasional nights on Stamford sofas again, commuting in an old Renault that Jimmy had given me during the short time I was separated from Joe, a generous gift surely meant to lure me back to him. It didn't. I was grateful, but not enough to be upfront with him when I went back to Joe. I never told him. It wasn't long before I quit my hostess job. I couldn't see Joe in Stamford and work in White Plains at the same time, could I? I'm not sure where Joe stayed when we weren't together. I didn't want to know.

After a quick check-in with my family on Christmas Eve, I drove to Georgia's in Redding in a snowstorm. I got lost on the way and had to find a pay phone outside a closed gas station to call Joe for directions. I was cold, wet, and exhausted by the time I finally got there.

"Sit here, sugar," Georgia said, and she sat me down on the raised fieldstone hearth in front of the fire. "And take this," and handed me a Dewar's on the rocks. The dampness from my hair and red flannel dress, which was soaked from where I had sat on a wet seat in the phone booth, made the air smell like wet dog. Or else it was a wet dog. Georgia and Cal had a good-natured German shepherd named Shanti, and he was spread out on the slate floor nearby.

I was just starting to get the chill out of my bones when Georgia sat in an upholstered chair across from me and hugged her hands together and stared at Joe. Cal grumbled something and went to the kitchen. Joe suddenly knelt down in front of me. I thought he was going to poke at the fire, but instead, he put his hand in his pocket and pulled out a ring.

"Will you marry me?" he asked.

I put my drink down and stared at the ring. "Oh," I said. "Oh."

It was only a little over three months since the night we met. I didn't know what to think. Marriage seemed square and somewhat irrelevant, the reason everyone at the Blue Note had laughed when he said he was going to marry me. In its most rigid form, it was an institution that turned women into their husband's chattel. But perhaps an interracial marriage was the ultimate rebellion? Without waiting for a yes or no, Joe took my left hand and slipped the ring on my finger. It did not fit. It was the ring Joe's father had given Georgia when she was seventeen years old, and although she was no bigger than I was, the ring was too large. She was already pregnant with Joe, so maybe she was retaining water. Who knows? I held my hand out carefully so the ring would not fall off and admired it. It was gold with two entwined hearts, like a double-ended arrow tied in a knot, with little diamond chips embedded in the hearts.

"Okay," I said, with a shrug. Georgia clapped her hands, and Cal came back from the kitchen with fresh ice in his drink and another grumble.

"I love you, Bunny Foo Foo," Joe said, using a name taken from a nursery rhyme he'd heard me recite to Kenny and Paula's little girl. I scowled at the endearment but said "I love you," back.

In high school, on the back pockets of a pair of jeans, I had elaborately embroidered the words *Le coeur a ses raisons que la raison ne connaît point.* The heart has its reasons that reason knows nothing of. I might have even been wearing them when I met Joe, and when the jeans wore out I kept the pockets. I still have them. Yet, in spite of what my pants said, there is still a nagging part of me that believes that our brains can decipher our hearts. Were Joe and I drawn to one another by the color of our skin? You betcha. Joe, as I was to discover, dated only white women. On my part, curiosity might explain the skin-deep attraction of a one-night stand, but not a two-year relationship. Rebellion is too pat, zeitgeist is too abstract, and romantic chemistry too complex to unpack. Although I do remember being drawn to Joe's voice, which was deep and emotive, as befitted the gospel singer's son, especially when he recited Shakespeare, which was more often than one would think. "To be, or not to be: that is the question," Joe would exclaim with drunken gusto. "Whether 'tis nobler in the mind to suffer the slings and arrows of outrageous fortune, or to take arms against a sea of troubles." Not content to just recite the lines, Joe, the princeling wannabe, would then interpret them as well, making a show of his liberal education. He gave Hamlet a racial spin, suggesting a tactical struggle between Martin Luther King Jr.'s civil disobedience and Black Panther violence. I remember being impressed, as I was the first night we met when he dropped Hamlet's heaven and earth line, even though later I realized it was no more Shakespeare than could be picked up in a Bugs Bunny cartoon.

I continued to poke at the bones of our love through the 80s and 90s while working on my undergraduate degree, taking night classes at Harvard

Extension, so that by the time my children were contemplating college I'd have a diploma to wave about like a flag. I was a social science major, with a focus on gender studies, so I was knee deep in French feminist theory and Lacan. At that time, I looked on my relationship with Joe as falling in love with the Other and contemplated that my real attraction to Joe was the distance between us. We were two opposing forces, and the tension that it created was the excitement we felt for one another.

It was an interesting intellectual exercise, but beyond all that, I was simply charmed, a delightful sensation that I now recognize as a warning bell. It was the charm I was dangerously receptive to. I have never liked labels, so I am not going to put one on Joe or anyone else in my life. A label like "narcissist," for instance, can rob a person of his or her humanity and condense them into a single pathological trait. "Grandiosity" is another word I don't like to use, so I won't. Instead, I will say that there are those who, when they turn their attention on you, pull you into the world they have created, and it is warm and intense. You feel so special, but you are only an accessory to their vision, not a person who might have a vision of her own. There is a theory that people are attracted to those with whom they can work out unresolved issues about one or both parents, and I could have been its poster child. I would have been attracted to Joe even if his skin was green, because he was just so damned familiar. Maybe we are all drawn to the person who has a lesson to be taught. But my being in love with the person I wanted him to be and not who he was only makes me one of the millions of people who fall in love every day not knowing that that is the name of the game.

We were engaged for the next year and nine months without ever making plans to actually get married, although Georgia and I would sometimes talk about dresses. Joe liked to think out loud about wedding presents. At the top of his registry was a small Derringer, a gun, without which one could not set up housekeeping, apparently. Not an interracial household at any rate. In many ways, it was amazing that we could talk about such a marriage in 1975, just eight years after the Supreme Court, in the Loving decision, made interracial marriages legal. Eight years.

———————

A FEW DAYS AFTER CHRISTMAS, but before New Year's, Joe and I were hanging out in Pleasantville at the bar owned by Aunt Ginny and Uncle Dave, who had recently retired from the NYPD. It was as if the 60s hangout scene got picked up out of their house and deposited in the bar. We had gone to Pleasantville to see friends of mine from high school who were home from college, living my phantom life. They talked about classes and dorms, papers and cafeteria food, the world I had opted out of, all of which now sounded pretty sweet. If my aunt and uncle were disturbed to see me there with a black man, they did not say anything to me, although I made sure Joe and I made no physical contact. If my aunt told my mother about him, I could say he was just a friend. I was all for civil rights and self-determination as long as it didn't get me into trouble. I had not yet understood that my hiding our relationship was a racist act in itself.

Joe found out from one of my friends that my parents had a billiard table and talked us all into going there. I must have had too much to drink, because I said, "Why not," knowing a fistful of reasons why not. We gathered up our coats, and in two separate cars, we headed a couple of blocks away to my parents'. I thought it went without saying that Joe was to make believe we were not a couple. Not only did I expect him to stay in his segregated box, but I assumed he would do it without even being told. We were engaged to be married, and I was still not prepared to tell my family. Yet I wore the ring on my finger.

The billiard table was not in the basement but in what had been the dining room, under a crystal chandelier. My mother was in the kitchen, and my father was, as was his habit, upstairs watching TV. I don't know whether my two younger siblings were home, but if they were, they didn't make their presence known. It was unusual to have people in the house not specifically invited by my mother, so everyone was keeping their heads down. That was my family in a nutshell.

I started to play eight ball with my friends and didn't notice that Joe, in his ongoing campaign to raise racial consciousness, had escaped from my watch and gone into the kitchen to chat with my mother. He might have been looking for a drink. She offered him a cup of tea, which he accepted, but it probably put him in a dangerous mood. At any rate, he said, "I'm going to marry your daughter."

I didn't know any of this until my mother appeared by my side and yanked me out into the living room. Joe was standing behind her with his teacup, smirking.

Oh shit. Instigating little bastard. That's what I thought then. But I knew him well enough at that point to know what he'd do. I was asking for it. No, I begged for it, motivated by a force I didn't even know existed, operating from anger I couldn't even touch. I was too cowardly to tell my parents myself, but I had created the opportunity for Joe to do it for me.

"Is it true?" she screamed. "Are you engaged to this . . ." and she struggled to find the words for Joe. "This *man*?" She pointed at Joe, who stood a foot away from the tip of her finger, leaning against the staircase, sipping his tea. I looked at him as if I were considering whether it was this man or some other one, as if it were a police lineup. It was hardly worth lying about now. I was afraid of my mother's anger, and even more afraid of what would happen if my father came downstairs, but I had my shield of righteousness.

"Yes," I said, and I held up my left hand as proof. The ring had been made to fit with white surgical tape, but it was still loose, so when my mother slapped me hard across the face, my whole body twisted, and the ring flew off my finger.

It's a cheesy metaphor, the ring leaving my body by the sheer force of my mother's fury, but this isn't a novel, so it's not like I can change it.

There was no time to look for the ring. I was chased out of the house. If my father heard what was going on downstairs, he never let on. He might have been hiding with my siblings. I don't know how I found my coat or how I made it to the car, but when I got outside, Joe was waiting for me with the car running. He was thrilled. He had dragged me from my parents and I let him. No. I had set him up to do it.

All in all, the evening had been no *Guess Who's Coming to Dinner?*

After I left, my poor friends, still clutching their pool cues, had to maneuver themselves out of the house with my mother, already looking for someone to blame, now directing her rage at them for letting me date Joe in the first place. As Joe and I drove to Stamford, I cried, but in many ways I was relieved that I didn't have to carry the lie around anymore. I was also relieved to be out of my mother's house for good, even though this meant being homeless again, my fate tied to a man as unanchored as I was. But I know this much now, and I suspected it even then: Joe and I would have fizzled out soon enough if left to our own devices. But having been pushed into a corner, he was the small plot of ground on which I could plant my flag.

———————————

MANY YEARS LATER, my sister, Pert, told me that later that same night, my mother sat her and my younger brother down. My older brother was long gone, having been forced out of the house in his own drama. Pert was around fourteen at the time, and my younger brother must have been eleven. "I have something terrible to tell you," my mother said, somberly. "Your sister is living with a black man."

There was a pause. "And?" Pert said.

My mother didn't speak to her for weeks, and she was no longer allowed to watch *The Jeffersons** on TV. The next day, I went back to the house to gather up the few things I was allowed to take. Joe must have made the call. I can't imagine myself picking up the phone. I gathered up my small pile of belongings, which my mother had collected and dropped on the floor downstairs, while she hyperventilated a string of invectives. I can't remember much of what she said, except that it was all attack. She did not want me to be with him, yet she did not ask me to stay. She was angry that I had hidden it from her, yet her overblown hysteria was proof why I had. Mostly, she screamed variations of "How could you do this?" "How could you do this to us?" and "How could you do this to me?" without ever saying what "this" was. It was clear she was furious at me for being with a black man, but she did not use any offensive language or refer to the color of his skin in any way. She did not bring up the fact that I was way too young to be marrying anyone, because she had been nineteen when she got married herself. She didn't know what to do, and since anger was her most easily accessible emotion, she grabbed at that. My most accessible emotion was fear. I doubt I said more than a few words. What was there to say? It was all true, I was engaged to Joe. He was waiting for me in the car, and I was afraid he'd come in and make things worse, as was his wont, so I quickly jammed everything into a pillowcase. Seeing that she was losing her audience, my mother got on the phone to my father, who was safely at work in the city and started yelling at him. I stood up, amazed to see my engagement ring, still with its surgical tape on, sitting on the marble fireplace mantle. I paused to put it back on, and my mother grabbed the opportunity to drop the phone, run across the room, and slap me across the face.

Goodbye, Mom. I am so out of there.

AFTER JOE AND I LEFT Pleasantville, we drove to Carol's on Court Street, where, exhausted and in tears, I threw myself on her sofa.

"Mind if we crash here for a few days?" asked Joe.

*The *All in the Family* spinoff about a prosperous black family.

Carol had never said no to Joe, and she did not this time either. "Of course," she said in her sleepy voice. She stood leaning against the living room door and lit a cigarette. As the smoke swirled around her, she examined the burning coal at its end. "Howie and Margo are moving into the apartment across the hall."

Joe looked at the door as if he were looking through it and frowned. "Hmm," he said. "Howie Zowie."

"I don't like it one bit, Joe," Carol said. "It's going to be trouble."

WHEN JOE AND I entered 1976, scrunched together as we were on Carol's sofa, we had no money, no apartment, no prospects, and no car. The Renault had died on the Merritt within days of leaving Pleasantville, and we did not have the money to have it towed or fixed. Joe sold the tires to a friend the next day, but the car was stripped by the time the friend got there. Joe hustled—meaning, he hung out in bars for a few days asking about cheap places to live. He found a room rental, courtesy of a pleasant Vietnam vet who was divesting his life of inessentials so he could find himself, or lose himself, by hitchhiking out West. The room was part of a three-bedroom apartment on the top floor of a wooden triplex on Crandall Street, right in downtown Stamford. One of the bedrooms was a sleeping porch that was sealed up with plastic in the winter, but we had a real room that looked out over an enclosed yard of dirty snow. It even came with a mattress on the floor that the vet left behind. Our roommates were two white guys, Mark and David. We lived there for nine months, and when I left, I did not think about that time of my life again until I started looking for Margo.

SINCE MY CALL to the Stamford police about Margo's case had yielded nothing but more questions, the next step was to read the Stamford *Advocate* from 1976, even though I did not completely trust what it had to say. I felt that whatever they had printed about Howie and Margo would have come through the filter of the police, but whether or not it was the truth, it was the recorded history. I was not much of a newspaper reader when this history was actually taking place. The only time I remember handling newsprint was looking for a job, and back then, the employment section in the classifieds was divided into "Men" or "Women," with only a couple of opportunities under the second, typist or waitress.

The older archives of the city's daily paper were not digitized, so to read the original articles about Margo's death I had to return to the city itself. Off to gather missing pieces. Off to make amends. Off to mend. When, in June 2002, I drove the four hours to Stamford, it was the first time I'd been back since early October 1976, when Joe and I moved to Westport, leaving Howie and Margo in the ground behind us. As I was driving around Stamford, trying to find the library in a city I barely knew anymore, I had to roll down the window for air. I felt that Joe was in my Subaru wagon next to me, and I couldn't breathe. I had internalized the lesson that just being seen in public with him could be a dangerous activity in itself. Driving, especially, put us at the mercy of the police. My eyes kept darting down the side streets, looking for the black-and-white cop cars, waiting for the damning blue flash of light. I actually glanced at my inspection sticker on the windshield to make sure it was up to date. After a few wrong turns, I arrived at the Ferguson Library without having been stopped. But of course. I was a middle-aged white woman in a station wagon, minding her own business.

The library is located at the intersection of Broad and Summer, in the few downtown blocks left standing after urban renewal. It has the traditional red brick walls, white fluted columns, and classic portico of early twentieth-century American civic architecture. One wing of the old building is now a Starbucks, a seamless marriage of municipal and commercial forces. I don't remember visiting the library or reading a single book the entire time I lived in Stamford, but I did, because I still have the library card. I found it in the same box with the bail bondsman's card, but obtaining the card might be as far as I got toward a reading life. It takes leisure time to read words, and a focused mind to process them. It takes a safe place to keep a library book, so it doesn't get mislaid, filched, or tossed out the window, because what are you doing reading that women's lib crap? Or honky bullshit.

Not that I ever saw Joe read a book either. For all the fuss he made over his elite education, he seemed indifferent to the written word, as if he had learned just about enough. No matter. Forget Joe. Here was history, and even though it was history through the distorted lens of the powers of the day, I would find the reports of her death that would bring her back to life. I would find the world we lived in.

Resurrection.

In the end, I would discover that you had to already know the story to find the story, but I knew nothing that first day at the library. I certainly didn't know that it would take many visits over several months to finish the first leg of my search (Note on kitchen counter: "Off to investigate a murder. Dinner in oven. Love, Mommy") with three children and a husband back in Massachusetts scratching their heads.

The microfilm machines and archives were in the musty basement of the Ferguson. Once I got settled with my coffee and notebook in front of the machine, the librarian asked, "Where do you want to start?" She had a drawer open with dozens of gray metal cannisters lined up like ammunition, each marked with the many weeks of 1976.

I looked at her blankly. Even though I had been mulling over Margo for a few years at this point, I hadn't a clue what month she died in. I couldn't even remember what season her murder took place. How can that be when it happened around the bicentennial? It should have been a flashing memory marker, but it wasn't. It's not that I was unaware of the event itself. I clearly recall *Her-story* on TV, one-minute PSA clips that aired all that year, highlighting women who had been neglected in America's history (his-story). Many of my peers knew exactly what they did during the celebration, and it was a frequent topic of conversation at the time. I remember a high school friend telling me that her family went to her father's office in the brand-new World Trade Center to watch the fireworks. As a rule, people celebrated with their families, and I was estranged from mine. Georgia probably went with Cal to a local Redding event, where Joe would not have been welcome. Talented black women, yes, their black sons, no. We went nowhere and did nothing. If that seems unlikely, consider this. The bicentennial was no big deal in much of the black community. Alex Haley's novel, *Roots*, which stirred up considerable interest in African American history, would not be released until September 1976, and the popular series was not aired until the following year. Before Vernon Jordan went off to be Clinton's soul mate, he was the executive director of the National Urban League, and in that capacity toured the country in the spring of 1976 to get the black community to participate in bicentennial festivities. He spoke in Stamford on June 17 to plead his case. He told the audience that they needed to be involved to remind the rest of the country that in 1776 only white Americans had been free—black people were still legal possessions.

How were they supposed to do that? Go out in the streets to proselytize about the plight of enslaved blacks in 1776? Then watch the fireworks?

Vernon was the "white man's tool" as Joe would say. Going along with the program meant condoning America's racist history, and Joe refused to celebrate it. We stayed home on the Fourth of July and watched an old movie on TV. A few years later, Vernon was shot in the back while climbing out of a white woman's car.

So, no, the bicentennial rang no bells for me. I had so few bells to begin with where Margo was concerned, she had been buried so completely in my psyche. I was fairly certain it was in 1976, but my first impulse was to think of the fall. Of course, the fall. Isn't that when everything is dying anyway? When Joe told me about Margo, I remembered that the pavement was wet, with dead leaves in the street and bunching up at the drains, but that must have been the result of a summer downpour, not autumn rain. Because if nothing else, I knew we were living on Crandall Street when Margo was killed. We had no home in the fall of 1975, and we were already in Westport in the fall of 1976. So, right off the mark, my memory had placed Margo's death in an impossible time. Even though I was actively searching for her, I couldn't seem to push her far enough away. I wanted to know how she died, and I was afraid of knowing. I didn't want it to be Howie because that would reflect poorly on interracial couples, but I really didn't want to discover it was someone who killed her for being with a black man. Then, as now, Margo and I would have been at real risk of being verbally and physically attacked on the street by any number of people: racists, white supremacists, police, even enraged family members, all of which touched on fears I tried to ignore during the time I was with Joe. There were less obvious dangers as well. When we threw away the societal restrictions and taboos to enter into those relationships, we had to discard all the rules. We were outside the gates in volatile times, often in poverty, which in itself is a serious threat to anyone. There were no guidelines and precious few examples. All we had were a handful of other such couples in Stamford to look to as an example in a world that had little use for us, black or white.

"I'll start at the beginning of the year, I guess," I said, and the librarian handed me a canister, then taught me how to thread the stiff plastic tape through the reels of the machine and read the dark, imperfect photocopies of the city's daily paper.

"These are the first few days of January," she said. "Then work your way down these rows, in this order. 1976 continues into the next drawer." She held her arms out toward the cabinet, looked at me, and smiled. "I hope you've got plenty of time."

————————————

I SAT IN FRONT OF that microfilm machine for many an hour, moving film though the cogs with a turn of a knob, each one holding only a few days of the paper. When I began, I thought I'd be quickly scrolling through the articles until I found a bow and arrow murder, but that wasn't the case. There was no way of finding Margo without sifting through all the pages, and I was mesmerized. The Stamford *Advocate* was preserved as printed, including ads. For all the rampant inflation, with oil quadrupling in price in 1973 and the cost of meat rising 40 percent between 1972 and 1973, life still seemed cheap, with sixty-nine-cent chuck at Bongiovanni's Supermarket and Max Factor lipstick for under a dollar at Genovese Drugs. I remembered many of the stores and the streets, but not how sordid it all was. Hardly a day went by that the paper didn't report on conflict-of-interest charges against city boards and agencies, serious shortages of low and moderate rentals in the city, with escalating accusations between tenants' associations and the housing authority, highlighted by a dead mouse presented to the authority. Most hurtful were the small, quotidian decisions of the local boards and councils, whose members did not seem to reflect too hard or long on who would suffer by their actions.

What was of particular interest scrolling though Stamford's past was to find out that Joe's paranoia about the police was not just legitimate but downplayed. It can't even be called paranoia when it's just the truth, and this was one filthy bunch of cops. In the February 1976 archives, I read that the new head of the vice squad was instructed to focus on narcotics and gambling on the police force. It was soon dismantled for lack of interest. In the same week, a woman was charged with killing her gambling boy-friend, a former policeman with a long rap sheet. In March, two officers faced criminal charges for alleged theft, and by the end of the month, Chief of Police Kinsella, of post office fame, was asked to step down by community leaders on charges of corruption. He declined.

That spring, in the buildup to the bicentennial, everything in town, from trash cans to fire hydrants was being painted red, white, and blue. The bi-centennial birthday ball was being planned at the Italian Center, the heart of city politics, but it was news of the police that filled the paper. Brutality accusations and other irregularities were commonplace, including an article about a cop using drugs at work and being allowed to remain on duty. The drug? Crystal meth. This was not the same incident that Joe was regaling his harem with back at the Blue Note months before, it was just one of many instances. There are more things in heaven and earth, as Hamlet would say. Oh, Joe, how could I have ever doubted you? The same article mentioned, in passing, that the water cooler at the police station was full of vodka, not water. Fueled on alcohol, they had quick draw contests in their backyards in densely populated neighborhoods. One of them shot himself and had to be hospitalized. By the end of May, the department as a whole was charged with unreasonable force by community activists, mostly church leaders. Going into June, the headline read, "Clergymen starting City watchdog group cite 'hidden deals' mob influence rumors." Soon after, a cop was suspended for drug use, and this was not even the crystal meth cop from May. In late June, two cops were found guilty of larceny for the theft of aluminum siding in the fall.

Aluminum siding? Who steals siding? The Stamford police were walking off with everything that wasn't tied down, with half-cocked pistols and drug-addled brains. I shook my head. It was a shameful thing, but police corruption was not what I was looking for. I was searching for Margo, so along with scanning for the words "murder" or "arrow," I paid attention to the almost daily racist reports, which seemed integral to our lives, although the headlines were often just stating the obvious. "Officer of fair housing says discrimination still exists." At a Pitney Bowes dinner, honoring a HUD representative, Sylvia Rosenfield stated that "discrimination is a very strong factor when it comes to obtaining a place to live in Stamford." James Blair, assistant secretary for equal opportunity at HUD, called the Merritt Parkway in Stamford a symbolic "Mason-Dixon line."

As humble as Crandall Street was, and it was very humble, Joe and I were lucky not to be in public housing. January 1976 was bitter cold. On the twenty-third of the month, the front page showed a photograph of a thermometer, the temperature minus four degrees. Day after day, the lead stories at the top half of the page were about the extreme weather, and under the fold were the small articles about public housing with no heat, burst water pipes, and a housing authority where no one picked up the phone. A headline read, "Pastor is seeking Wormser ouster." The pastor was Rev. Ralph Johnson, the minister of the predominantly black Baptist church, helping his congregation to organize against housing authority director Margot

Wormser, whom he charged with "neglect and insensitivity to the basic needs of the Southfield Village residents."

Wormser told a reporter she never heard from any of the residents, which was exactly their point. The authority hadn't answered the calls about no heat or the subsequent calls about no water when all the pipes burst. Housing authority chairman Anthony Marrucco said it was all "a lot of baloney" and that he hadn't heard any complaints either. The housing authority was supposed to hold a meeting to discuss these accusations, but it was cancelled due to severe weather. In an article a day later, Wormser and Marrucco blamed all the problems on the telephone company. In response to this, the head of the Moderate Income Tenant's Advisory Committee said Marrucco was full of baloney.

All this baloney, but not a single slice for student lunches. The school board celebrated the opening of the bicentennial year by voting down the hot lunch program, often the only balanced meal poor (read: black) children ever received. Alone, this seemed to be merely an austerity measure taken in difficult times. But no. There was money for food in the budget, it was just not going to the kids. Later in January, the headline read, "School officials dine out; public tab $2200." The board was running a hot lunch program of their own. They took each other out to fashionable restaurants and charged it to the city. They flew off on $7,500 convention junkets to Miami. They spent hundreds of city dollars on flowers and jewelry that they gave to each another. They loved one another. They chewed the fat over a cup of java. One thousand dollars had been spent just to run the two coffee urns in the office of the school board's community relations director. But there was not a penny for food for the kids.

It was a recipe for trouble and trouble happened, with sports events turning explosive all over town. During this time, Joe and I went to see a Golden Gloves competition in a school auditorium. It was pretty cute—small boys with huge boxing gloves tied to their wrists, wearing oversized mouth guards, inexpertly pounding away at one another with parents screaming encouragement. Older kids had some style, and the teenagers were sublime. Audience and participants were about 90 percent black. I was the only white female, or as we used to say, I felt like the middle of an Oreo cookie. But it was a congenial crowd.

Not so elsewhere. In February, a wrestling match between Stamford Catholic and Westhill High—a fairly new school in North Stamford that drew students from all over the city—broke out into a fight involving up to seventy-five wrestlers, parents, and spectators, ignited by racial slurs. The police had to be called in, and more than a few people were hospitalized. Events like this were becoming the norm, and city officials scrambled to say it had nothing to do with race.

With no lunch program, the kids in the city started getting pretty cranky at the end of the day. In the same month, at Westhill High, students beat up their bus driver. It was raining, and the school buses didn't show up, so the kids packed the only one that did. When the white bus driver tried to regulate the numbers, about thirty of the "almost exclusively black" students yelled at her, making racial remarks, before attacking her physically. The board of education president, Ellen Camhi, told the reporter that the beating was because Westhill was "populated with rich whites and poor blacks. The white kids hate the blacks and the black kids hate the whites. It's too bad. But the kids aren't to blame completely either, because they get it from home."

Let's not mince words. Camhi must have thought better of this comment, or at least she did after someone seemed to have lectured her on the newly minted concept of political correctness, because a few days later the headline read, "Mrs. Camhi modifies 'racism' quote." She then said that incidents at Westhill resulted from "a complex of problems which exist in society as a whole as well as the school, and that it would be incorrect to blame any trouble at the school on race prejudice alone."

Was I aware of race riots and housing protests going on around us? Vaguely. These incidents were not so much a topic for discussion as a presence in our lives. Someone might say, "Did you hear about . . . ?" and would be cut off with a groan. Discrimination, violent racial flare-ups, what else was new? You didn't need a newspaper to tell you why you couldn't find a decent place to live, or why the police stopped you for the hell of it. It was not news, it was life.

In early June 1976, tensions between the city and black parents escalated. Soon, the board would wish they had their overcrowded bus problems back. HEW* released a mandate for the city to desegregate the city's elementary schools. In response, the school board announced a plan that inflamed the

*The U.S. Department of Health Education and Welfare, which reorganized in 1979 into two separate entities, the Department of Education and Health and the Department of Human Services.

black community. They voted to ship black kids out of the inner city to what one protester called "fringe" schools, with no reciprocal busing of white kids to the predominantly black schools downtown. The board dared not ask white kids—their own children—to do what it was demanding of the black students. Since there was no other way to integrate these downtown schools, they closed them. The lone black member of the board of education pleaded with the other members not to pass the plan. They did it anyway.

Black parents went to the streets in protest. One of the signs read, "Board of Education has no respect for Black Children." It was a far cry from the education that Joe and Howie had received, when catch-up was the name of the game in many communities, and every effort, at least for some, was made to level the playing field. But by the 70s, the federal government had taken on a bigger role in enforcing civil rights legislation, which must have felt like an affront to local boards, who balked at being told what to do and for whom. Stamford had its own agenda, with an eye toward a citywide school system that would be palatable to incoming executives and their families.

A federal civil rights committee gave the Stamford Board of Education some free advice: the board should hire some minority teachers, give more encouragement to black students, and study why so many blacks were in low-ability groups. The board members decided to hire their own consultant and then took each other out to lunch.

———————————

I'M SURE I SERVED many a plate of osso buco to the board members while they helped one another modify their racist statements over lunch. Soon after moving to Crandall Street, I had picked up a daytime shift at a nice Italian restaurant across town that catered to just that sort of clientele. I was able to get the job because the Vietnam vet whose room we took over wanted to sell us his yellow VW too. Joe was able to get a loan from his old friend at the bank, and we were mobile again.

Within the first month, the VW lost its front hood when it popped up in my face on I-95 while I was doing seventy. It was unlike me to be speeding (the limit in those gas-conscious days was fifty-five), but I was fighting with Joe and not paying attention. He laughed when it happened, as if this was a sign that he was right and I was wrong, laughing even as I was driving blind, while he leaned out the window to wave other cars away so we could pull over. The metal was twisted beyond repair, so he undid the remaining hinge and left the hood by the side of the road. The engine was in the back, so with the hood missing, the trunk was an open bucket to the world. Who knew that was illegal? We got stopped within hours, and Joe bought a cheap red replacement at a junkyard. It was a bicolor car from then on, but it made it possible for me to get the job at the Italian restaurant.

In the first week, the owner announced to us, his waitstaff, that he would break our fingers if we stole any shrimp. I shrugged it off. It never occurred to me to steal his pink rubbery shrimp, but the other waitress was stunned and quit right then and there. She said she would never work with a threat of violence over her. I thought she was being thin-skinned. It was just one of those things people said. Over time, I realized, no they didn't. Order didn't have to be maintained with threats, but it was how I was raised, with a continuous refrain of dire warnings. The ground rules at our house had always been that we were not to upset my mother or we'd pay the price, but that was a Sisyphean task because she got hysterical at the least little thing. I kept my head down. Because of this, I was considered the good one, but the truth was, I wasn't very good. I was frightened.

It was Joe who encouraged me to speak up for myself and call him on his shit. I was never frightened of him, not even when he was drunk, so, as if I were making up for lost time, we fought constantly. We especially fought after visiting his mother, where there was too much Dewar's and too little splash. On the way out the door, she'd give him his mail. He'd toss the bills away but kept letters from old girlfriends who only knew how to find him through Georgia. One night, when we got home, I read one of these letters. It was from California, and this woman I'd never heard of before wanted Joe to fly out and see her. And she'd pay his way.

"Without me?" I asked. "Where do I fit into this?" And the next thing I knew, we had on our full battle fury and I was leaving him. I was out in the backyard, and Joe was trying to get me back into the house. I was screaming for him to let me go.

"Do you want to bring the pigs?" he asked.

I did. At that moment I most certainly wanted the police to come so I could have a witness to his careless treatment of me. In the end, I went back inside, but not without a struggle.

Was that me? Was that really me?

On the second floor lived plump Mrs. Cornaro. She was recently divorced, and when we passed her apartment going upstairs to ours, we often heard her play, and play again, Gladys Knight's "Midnight Train to Georgia." The next day, as I was leaving for work, Mrs. Cornaro was sitting on her landing with a cup of coffee and mentioned, with a laugh, seeing Joe and me fighting in the yard the night before. "You two looked like you were having a time of it," she said, and seemed almost wistful.

*P*USHING THROUGH the microfilm at the Ferguson, I slogged my way, month by month to the summer of 1976. By then, I was working as a teller at the Mechanics & Farmers Bank in Old Greenwich, one of the many banks that would later go belly-up in the savings-and-loan crisis of the early 90s due to imprudent lending. It was a pretty funny bank to be in Old Greenwich, since neither mechanics nor farmers could have ever afforded to live there. I had taken the job for health insurance because I needed to have a deviated septum fixed, a surgery fad once thought to cure allergies.* And it was better money than I made before, so with Joe's odd jobs and my paycheck, we were able to make the rent and buy a few groceries. It was a stable time of our life together. Not so with Stamford. The cannisters continued to reveal more of the city's moral and ethical collapse, woven seamlessly between the ongoing saga of urban renewal and fires. Then, like a shot across the screen, there was the headline: "Mystery shrouds finding of body." A female body had been found on Wednesday, July 14, 1976, when the White family, searching for paupers' graves, smelled "something foul" in the air. It was reported in the Thursday edition of the Stamford *Advocate* on July 15. It had to be Margo. It was the first mention of her, or more specifically, her body, since no one except her killer, or killers, knew it was her yet. Sitting alone in the basement of the Ferguson Library, I felt my skin turn cold, as if I half expected never to find her, as if it had all been some crazy dream from long ago. I felt it more keenly this time around because I had never allowed myself to feel it before.

*In an episode of *Six Feet Under*, a woman, standing in line to get into a Rosie O'Donnell show taping, bleeds out and dies from this operation, which she too had had decades before. I didn't sleep for weeks.

I put aside all the corruption and real estate drama and began to follow Margo. What I didn't know yet was that in the end any path I took would lead to the same place.

———————————

I DID NOT SEE the "Mystery shrouds finding of body" headline in its time. If Joe knew a woman's body had been found, and I'll bet he did, he did not share that information with me. My coworkers at the bank never mentioned a dead body in Stamford either, yet they all knew I lived there. It was as if in the violent 70s we had become numb to bodies popping up in odd places. So, as I sat in the Ferguson Library reading the article, it was all new to me. In a press conference, Captain Thomas O'Connor, who was heading the investigation, announced the "nightmarish discovery" of a partially decomposed body of an unidentified woman at the abandoned potter's field off Scofield-town Road. "We were aware of the putrid odor of decay," said Mrs. William White, the high school teacher's mother. "But knowing the grounds, we thought it must have been a dead animal. Then we saw the newly turned earth—and the arm."

Captain O'Connor theorized that an animal had exposed the limbs of the body while digging at the makeshift grave. The corpse was covered in only a few inches of dirt. There were no visible signs of foul play either on the body or near the grave, but O'Connor described the situation as being "definitely a suspicious death, and we are investigating the possibility of homicide."

When I read the words, "no visible signs of foul play," I wondered, as I sat staring at the screen, if this Jane Doe was really Margo after all. I knew so little, but I knew she had been shot with an arrow. How could there be no signs of *that*? But this was before I understood the extent of the decomposition and the time that had passed. I'd always assumed she'd been shot, discovered, and identified all in one day or night, and that was how I remembered her murder over the years. Even that she'd been buried was news to me— I had always imagined her out in the open where she was felled, a crazed murderer running from the crime as concerned law enforcement arrived quickly on the scene. But when I read the physical description, such as it was, I knew it had to be Margo. "The body was of a woman with strawberry blond hair who was about five feet eight inches tall. It was clothed in blue jeans, a blue and white blouse and a single black cloth sandal."

The body. It. Cinderella has lost her martial arts slipper, which we all wore back then, sold cheaply at head shops. The prince arrived in the guise of the medical examiner, who couldn't even tell her age because her face had rotted away. Sitting there in the Ferguson basement, my brain was still not properly computing the words "putrid odor" and "partially decomposed." I did not absorb the underlying meaning of the story, that Margo had been dead for so long she'd become faceless. My defense system was still on high alert.

The medical examiner guessed she'd been dead for one to two weeks. "One to two weeks," I said out loud, and began to wonder again if this was really Margo. Had she been missing? Why hadn't I known that? Captain O'Connor told the reporters that an autopsy was scheduled the following day, and the police were reviewing a list of missing persons, six of whom were Stamford-area women who fit the general description of the discovered body.

A whole list. Let's consider, for a moment, these women. Six on the list fit the description, implying a longer list of those who did not. The number tells a story of the times. What with women's liberation and the human potential movement in general, the 70s was a decade of diaspora of women from their homes, following the wave of teenage runaways in the 60s. Leaving husbands and parents, they hit the road, too old to be runaways and not officially missing, just gone, back to the land, run off with other women, or just run off. They wanted to drop the labels of "wife," "daughter," or "mother" and just be human, in search of that elusive something, that promise of freedom that still hung in the air, that other word for nothing left to lose. But too many were like domestic pets set free in the wilderness with no skills to deal with predators and sometimes ended up as body dumps by the side of the road.

Margo had never made it to the list because she was not reported missing. I learned later that her step-father had helped her move from Stamford to Norwalk, so there was some communication with her family. They knew she had left Howie, so they probably thought she was out of danger. If they had read about the discovery of a young woman's body in the Stamford *Advocate*, they would not have immediately thought it had anything to do with Margo. In those days of landlines and long waits for installation, they would have just assumed she was waiting for her phone to be connected before they heard from her. They were probably simply happy she was finally free of Howie.

Let's say that back in July 1976, I had happened on this newspaper edition and read about the anonymous Jane Doe. Would I have felt anything beyond the normal revulsion of such a nightmarish discovery? Perhaps I would have wondered about the safety of that area of town or considered the possibility of a random killer, in the way that any woman's murder was cause for fear and alarm for half the population. You can be killed just for being female.

Who might be next? But would I have felt it had any personal connection to me? I knew so few women in Stamford, it was unlikely I would have thought it might be someone I knew. What would be the chances of that? No. I would have just shaken my head and sighed. What a world.

Other people reading this article knew right away it was Margo.

———————————

AT FIRST, the reporting was all shock and candor. The reporters rubbed their hands together and began their work. They held nothing back. Dead bodies sold papers, those of white women especially. They had Dead White Woman Fever, as James Ellroy would say.* They were not looking away from the "horrible-horrible" sight, as the traumatized White family described it, even as I averted my gaze. I barely scanned the words, afraid of their power. I did not even notice that the article had a photo, beneath it and to the right, until I examined the printout in the safety of my home. The photographer took a shot of three policemen, two of them bare-chested in the unrelenting heat, wearing gas masks. The dead are so powerful, masks are the only way the living can interact with them. The officers are looking down at the ground with their hands on their hips and appear to be shrugging.

There were not that many murders a year in Stamford. Five? Six? Just slightly above the national rate, higher than it is today. Few enough that a dead body should have been big news. Yet it was under the fold. The lead story of the day was the Democratic National Convention taking place in Madison Square Garden, where Southern boy Jimmy Carter was nominated as the 1976 Democratic presidential candidate. Perhaps there was so little talk about the gruesome discovery because it had been subsumed by historical events. The photo above the article, "Mystery shrouds finding of body," is that of the convention crowd, thousands of people holding "Carter" signs with hand-drawn hearts, some with arrows slicing right through them.

Did I mention that Howie's last name was Carter? A sick private joke among the dead.

I wish I could have cast a vote for Jimmy Carter. He was a good man, but I had somehow missed the Connecticut presidential primary in May. I didn't even vote in my first presidential election. Having arrived too late to enroll in Westport, I didn't make the effort to return to Stamford to cast a ballot. By that time, I was wondering what any of it had to do with me.

*James Ellroy, *My Dark Places* (New York: Knopf, 1996).

O N JULY 16, 1976, the day after the article about the discovery of the mystery body appeared, the coverage continued on the front page, full of shock over what had been found in her heart. The headline read, "Hunting arrow was used to kill unidentified woman." An arrow? How bizarre is that? The feathered death, like something from a gothic fairy tale. It was downright martyrish. The article went on to describe where the body had been found at the potter's field, about nine paces from a narrow dirt road that bisected the lot. "Police said there was evidence that cars had used the road during the summer because the grass was flattened." The abandoned Old Scofieldtown Road had once led to the Stamford branch of the University of Connecticut,* and school employees said it was sometimes used by students who wanted a secret place to drink and use drugs. "It is also reportedly used as a lover's lane." The road had been blocked off when the city stopped using the potter's field in 1970, but the barricade was down when the body was found, and no one knew how long it had been gone.

The autopsy was performed by Elliot Gross, MD. If I tried to use that name for a coroner in a novel the critics would call it a farce. Never mind that the man who found Margo is White or that the man who made millions from Stamford's redevelopment is Rich. The Ferguson Library? As in the Ferguson race riots of 2014? For real? The city is like a medieval allegory. No matter. At the time of Margo's autopsy, Dr. Elliot M. Gross was already a dead-body celebrity. As Connecticut's chief medical examiner, he had done Martha Moxley's, the Greenwich teenager bludgeoned to death with a golf club in 1975. Michael Skakel, cousin of Robert F. Kennedy Jr., was accused

---

*The campus has since moved downtown, replaced by Rippowam Middle School.

of the crime. Gross's missteps in that case were cited in Skakel's trial twenty-five years later, when Skakel was convicted for the murder. Then, late in 2013, a judge set Skakel free, saying that he was poorly represented in his trial by his lawyer.* Among other reasons, the lawyer had failed to point out to the jury that there were two black youths from the Bronx in Greenwich that night, one a former classmate of Skakel's at the Brunswick School, a cousin of Lakers player Kobe Bryant.

Gross would go on to become New York City's medical examiner and performed John Lennon's autopsy in 1980. In 1987, Mayor Koch fired him over the autopsy of Michael Stewart, a black Brooklyn graffiti artist who died in police custody in 1983. Dr. Gross reported that the death was from cardiac arrest, but the examiners hired by the Stewart's family insisted it was death by excessive police force. Gross had removed and hidden the eyes so that the other examiners could not determine death by strangulation. Gross eventually retired under a cloud for misdiagnosing a case in New Jersey in 2002 that had sent an innocent white man to prison for murdering his wife.

But Gross was still at the beginning of his career with Margo. The morning after her body was exhumed, he got down to his unpleasant job. What could be worse than being in the presence of a human body in the full unfolding of its decomposition? She was barely holding together. Gross and his assistants insulated themselves with gloves, respirators, evidence bags, and professional distance. First, they snipped off bandanas from around the neck and wrist, then removed a blue-faced Timex watch with roman numerals, a brown leather bracelet, a silver ring made from thirteen interlocking circles, and a double-edged razor blade on a heavy link chain around her neck.

We all wore the puzzle rings of interlocking circles, but what seems out of place was the "ornamental razor blade." What is ornamental about a razor blade? Does it mean the edges were made dull? Other than shaving, there are two images that a razor evokes. One is cocaine. It was not the major recreational drug it would become in the affluent 80s, but it was around. Maybe in a business relationship Margo had with Howie, the street doctor, coke was her department. From her Darien years, she would have had access to a rich clientele who could afford it. Maybe she was boldly advertising her wares with the razor around her neck, like the retail signs of preliterate populations: a sheep for wool, a knife for butcher, a blade for coke. Jewelry maker that she was, she might have even made it herself.

*The conviction was reinstated in 2016 and reversed again in 2018.

The other image a razor blade conjures up is suicide. Or maybe it just reads, "keep the fuck away from me." At any rate, it's a strange and provocative piece of jewelry, a detail that would allow most women reading the newspaper to breathe a sigh of relief. We were always looking for reasons a woman might have been murdered, other than our common gender. We so want to blame the victim for what happened to her, when we know the problem is almost always men.

The autopsy continued. With surgical scissors and tweezers, Dr. Gross peeled off her clothes. Blue jeans and a green halter top. No undergarments. There are changes in opinion over the color of the top, which had been described in the previous article as blue and later as striped. It was as rotten as Margo's skin, perhaps in shreds, and certainly black with blood, but they are not sure of that part yet. When they have her naked, they look for any identifying marks, but there are no tattoos, no scars. She has recent damage to her shoulder, but she'd never had surgery. She had never been opened up, until now.

Carefully, using saws, knives, and rib spreaders, they splayed her torso. Inside, they counted the microbes, maggots, and worms, the coroner's friends who tell him how long she'd been dead and how long she was in the ground, which in this case were two very different figures. "The coroner estimated that the woman had been murdered about two weeks ago and had been in the grave for several days."

It is a bizarre detail with a limited number of explanations and begs the question of where her body was all that time, out of the ground. When the medical examiner arrived at the potter's field to take photographs, he would have also taken soil samples to indicate how much "human" had melted into the earth, telling him how long she'd been in that spot: Three days. And yet, according to the paper, the police were fairly certain she'd been murdered near the site of burial. The newspaper never made anything of this discrepancy, even though it was repeated in a number of articles. The reporter didn't ask the police where they thought she'd been in that time, or if they asked, they didn't print the answer. No one remarked on how puzzling it was.

Yet it is unlikely she had been buried anywhere before she was placed where she was found in her potter's field grave. The coroner did not indicate that the earth on Jane Doe was anything other than the earth that had surrounded her for those three days. Which means she must have been unburied for over a week.

While I was researching the original 1976 articles about Margo's murder, I looked beyond Stamford and found short pieces in other area papers. Their reporting seemed to be lifted directly from the *Advocate* articles, except for one, the *Bridgeport Post*. It must have sent its own reporter to the press conference, because that article differed in one slight way: "'We feel she was put here for some ulterior motive,' Detective Captain Thomas O'Connor, of the Stamford Police Department said today."

Put there? An ulterior motive? You mean, make it appear as if you were trying to dispose of a body, but you actually had some other reason to leave it where you did? Almost as if you wanted the body to be found.

———————————

THE CORONER CONTINUED his work, slicing open her stomach and examining the contents, a last meal of undigested fried chicken and coleslaw. There was gouged flesh higher up on the torso, and once the ribs were moved aside, Dr. Gross found the triple-pronged arrowhead embedded in Margo's heart. So much for "no signs of foul play" from the first article, which goes to show the extent of the rot. She'd been shot in the chest with a bone-splitting broadhead arrow used for big game. Not a slender Valentine's triangle, but a two-inch, three-bladed monster of ammunition. The arrow had severed the aorta before lodging in the left lung. It was removed "from one of the wounds."

One? *One* of the wounds?

"Police theorize that the murderer broke the arrowhead from the arrow shaft while attempting to remove it from the victim. No object was found in the second 'penetrating wound' Dr. Gross said."

The second penetrating wound. As I read the words, I wrapped my arms around my own ribs. I was alone in the library basement, as I usually was, but it was the first time I really noticed. There were two puncture wounds in Margo's body.

What sort of accident was that?

*T*HAT SECOND ARROW shot in Margo's body ripped a large hole through one of my theories, the one where Howie might have killed Margo by accident in some sick game. She was shot twice right over her heart. Margo's death was not an accident of any kind. It was not even an act of passion. Two shots are target practice. And it's mother-fucking cold.

Dr. Gross determined that one arrow had been pulled out, but when the killer shot her again, the arrow got stuck and had to be broken off. What a messy business that must have been. It is not impossible that the same arrow could have made both punctures if someone yanked it out and tried again. Maybe Margo was taking too long to die. Or the murderer took another shot, just for the sport. Or let someone else take a turn.

If mutilation is a sick language, what does an arrow through the heart mean? What do two?

One for hate and the other for love?

My other theory, that Margo could have died from an accidental drug overdose and then was shot with an arrow, no longer held water either. Margo died of the arrow wounds, not drugs. The autopsy revealed no toxins in her system, so that scenario was crossed off the list.

Whoever killed her meant to kill her. My story had to change again, but I didn't know in what direction. I wasn't ready to definitively pin it on Howie. I was still clutching one of my original three theories, that Margo had been killed by a random, quiver-carrying psychopath and that it was a mere co-incidence that Howie once expressed a desire to kill someone with a bow and arrow. I was trying to keep an open mind, but it wasn't looking good for Howie. The closer I got to that conclusion, the less enthusiastic I was feeling about my mission.

JUST THINKING ABOUT all this makes me want to crawl out of my skin. I want to get out of the 70s, away from the dead body for a bit. Let's say it's somewhere in the mid-80s. I had children of my own at that point, making my mother a grandmother. Except she wouldn't let anyone call her Grandma. It might have been her vanity, or she might have associated that name with her own mother, whom she did not care to be linked with. Her grandchildren call her Mu-Mu, a name she culled from the Mary Tyler Moore Show. She likes TV. She prefers a world where you can switch channels when you don't like what you're seeing.

One day, she came up from Pleasantville to visit my family in Massachusetts, where I have lived since 1979. The two of us had gone shopping, and I was driving with my mother in the passenger seat. She was always in the passenger seat because she never learned to drive. She tried, for a while. As bait, my father even promised to buy her an old Rolls Royce Silver Cloud to park in the driveway of the mansion they bought in the late 60s, a move on up from our first house in Pleasantville, a white Victorian with a mansard roof, just like the one in *The Addams Family*. The new house was smaller than the mansion next door, but still a mansion, which means it was built not just for size but for show. It was set up on a hill with an expanse of white stucco broken up by the architectural motifs of the Edwardian era: deep porch, attached gazebo, port cochere. Two staircases were de rigueur in a house such as this, a grand one for the owners and a dark, narrow one for the servants, which we did not have. Classy, is how my mother referred to it. The ruling class and the other class. It is what Joe and my mother had in common— no, they had quite a bit in common, but I won't go into that here. Suffice it to say that it was a house Joe would have gladly chosen for himself.

But there would be no classy accessory until she got her driver's license. My father was not getting her a car she couldn't drive, but she failed repeatedly to get her license. She blamed it on growing up in the Bronx, where everyone used public transportation, and there is some truth in that. Her many driving instructors blamed it on the fact that she got hysterical in the driver's seat and put her hands to her face when a car was coming. She could not bear to look. She let everyone else look instead and left it up to them to yank the car to safety.

Back in the car, in the mid-80s, apropos of nothing, my mother asked, "Did you know that Grandma died of alcoholism?"

"Of course I knew."

How could I not? The woman walked around with a Ballantine Ale in her hand all day. The older cousins laughed about it, so we, the little ones, did too, even though we weren't sure what we were laughing about. What none of us knew then, but we do now, is that she poured a shot of Wild Turkey in every can to turn up the heat.

"I didn't," she said, and looked away, as if she still could not believe it. She is a beautiful woman, and even as she turned away in confusion, she kept her chin lifted, her expression thoughtful. Her mother was born in Ireland, but her father was first-generation German, and that's the nationality she identifies with, claiming the high Aryan cheekbones and blond curly hair. When I was young, she pointed me in the direction of my father's side of the family, pure Irish, she'd say, and she meant it as no compliment.

"I only just found out she drank," she said. "Uncle Bill told me."

"Stop it," I said. Uncle Bill was her older brother, my mother the baby. Aunt Ginny was the oldest, and Aunt Pat, Denise's mother, was just a little older than my mother. Uncle Bill knew, and he lied about his age to escape to the navy at sixteen. Aunt Pat claimed not to know, even though Denise remembered being on the bus with her and Grandma. It was a rare day out of the apartment for Grandma, who was agoraphobic as well as alcoholic, and Aunt Pat had to fix her hair because it was drunkenly askew. But Aunt Ginny knew Grandma tippled, and her job as the oldest daughter was to keep the world from finding out.

"Your mother walked around with a beer in her hand all day," I said to my own mother. "How can you not have known?"

She put her hands up. "I just didn't."

In another mother-daughter conversation going on back in the Bronx, Denise asked her mother why she thought Grandma's hair needed fixing on that bus?

Aunt Pat shook her head. She just didn't put the pieces together.

There you have it. You can see something your whole life and not know what you're seeing. It is unrecognizable, even if it has always been there, reaching out, trying to break through the surface. If you'd asked me while I was with Joe whether he was an alcoholic, I would have scoffed. He liked his cocktails, that's all. And if you'd asked me at the same time, and for decades after, who killed Margo, I would have simply shrugged.

How much evidence was it going to take to make me remove my hands from my face?

BACK AT THE Ferguson Library, I scrolled to the next day in the archives and found Margo's ongoing story on page four, with the headline "Police fail to dig up new leads in bow and arrow murder here." The police released no new information on the murder investigation except to say they were trying to trace the retailer who sold the arrowhead that was removed from the mystery woman's chest. "The captain could report only that he had found very few sporting goods stores in the area sell such arrows and that nothing new had been learned from the statements."

That was on a Saturday, and the next paper was on Monday, July 19. On page four of that day's paper was the first mention of Margo, the person, as opposed to a body. "Murder victim identified; probe goes on."

———————

JOE AND I HAD just the one car, so either I took the VW to the bank or Joe dropped me off and picked me up. On Monday, July 19, he pulled our red-hooded yellow bug up to the curb and tossed the newspaper in my lap before I even got the car door closed. It was the paper with the "Murder victim identified" headline.

"Dig it," he said, not looking at me as he drove off. "It's Margo."

As there was no picture to go with the article, it took a minute for the words on the page to sink in. Margo? Our Margo? My eyes scanned for information, but I did not register any of it. My mind could not hold the words "murder victim" and someone I knew in the same thought. I hadn't known that a rotting Jane Doe had been found a few days before, not having read any of the articles about the mystery body, so I was totally unprepared for the news.

An "anonymous male" had called both the police and Margo's mother on Friday night, saying that the physical description of the woman and the jewelry seemed to match Margo. Her mother and stepfather identified the effects, and dental charts supplied by her Darien dentist confirmed her identity. Captain O'Connor said the victim formerly lived on Court Street in Stamford but had moved to Norwalk during the last week in June. He said police now had evidence that Margo was alive on Saturday, July 3, when she stayed for the weekend with Stamford friends.

Whoever the anonymous male was had to have been someone who knew that Margo was even missing. Who would have had the telephone number for Margo's mother, or even her last name, which was not Margo's? Other than an intimate, it is information that an employer might have had. But she was not currently employed, at least not in the conventional sense, although she had once been. "'We know she worked as a waitress for a time, for a local delicatessen,' Capt. O'Connor said." But if the connection was as innocent as all that, why anonymously? It was almost as if someone was getting impatient for her body to be identified. That "ulterior motive" thing.

"Formerly lived on Court Street." That was news to me. Until I read those words, I didn't know that Margo had moved from Court Street in late June. The article did not state whether she moved alone or with her boyfriend or what. Captain O'Connor was not forthcoming. "Now we have something to go on, and we're backtracking to find anyone who knew her."

Well, how about publishing a photo of her then? It's bad enough that Margo was portrayed only as a victim, with no backstory of her life, nothing to make her real in the minds of the readers. It did not even say that she'd grown up in Darien, right next door. Understandably, her mother might not want to release a photo of her, because with it she'd be releasing any hopes and dreams she'd once had for her daughter. But it seems odd that the paper couldn't have at least scrounged up a yearbook portrait. Wouldn't a picture of Margo in the newspaper have helped with the investigation, to "find anyone who knew her." And with the article buried on page four, they weren't going to find out who murdered her that way.

"Who could have done this?" I asked in horror, holding the *Advocate* at arm's length—the same question I'd be asking Denise twenty-five years later. Joe didn't answer me, but I did not hear that silence then. If he had known that a mystery body had been found the week before, he didn't let on now. It was more of a rhetorical question anyway. I was not expecting an answer, since it never occurred to me he might know or even suspect who had. I read into his silence that he was lost in thought about who could have done it. And deep down, I didn't want an answer. That would have made her murder too real and would have exposed my own vulnerabilities. The silence between me and Joe spoke volumes. What if Margo had been killed for being with a black man?

Today I would instantly think that the boyfriend did it, but not that day as I sat in the car holding the newspaper. What I didn't know then, but do now, is that when women are killed, it is more often than not at the hands of a partner. In my willful innocence at the time, in my desperate need to see my life as safe and well within the range of normal, I had convinced myself that no one would kill the one he loved. When in fact, without a financial incentive, who else would bother? That Margo might have been targeted for being part of an interracial couple was something I could not even look at.

I only let my mind consider the possibility of random violence, the catch-phrase of the day. It was a phrase that gained more traction as the Son of Sam killings began a few days later, when a white man in the Bronx pulled a gun from a paper bag and started shooting and continued to shoot for over a year. As was the case with Ted Bundy, who was on the first of his many trials right then, he preferred girls with long brown hair (raise your hand if you had long brown hair in the 70s) who reminded him of a former girlfriend, but we didn't know that then. We were all equally at risk. It takes time to see an underlying pattern, to understand what any particular act of violence is all about. What made Margo's murder different from the many others of the day was that she had been shot to death with an arrow.

An arrow. An arrow is anything but random or even spontaneous. Death by arrow is so medieval. Think of Robin Hood, the great equalizer, powerful symbol of the oppressed, stepping out from behind a tree in Sherwood Forest with his manly longbow. He robbed from the rich to give to the poor while Maid Marion blushed in admiration from the castle parapet. But time and technology move on. The arrow becomes history. Consider the classic Western flick, where the primitive weapon is no match for the guns of the white man in his wholesale slaughter of a race. But there has to be just cause. White men are not land-grabbing monsters! Honest. To prove it, in the opening scene we hear the whiz of a speeding arrow as it sends a cowboy flailing backward off his horse. In the carefully constructed myth of the American West, the Indian must shoot first. He must be the instigator in his own destruction.

Or as Kafka once wrote, it is enough that the arrows fit exactly in the wounds that they have made.

———————————

JOE DROVE FROM Old Greenwich to Stamford on back roads, wet with rain, passing Selleck Avenue, his old neighborhood, where he and Georgia had lived with his grandparents. Georgia had brought her mother and father up from Alabama to watch over her only child while she worked at the hospital, then later when she worked two jobs, the hospital during the day and New York jazz clubs at night, and later still, when she went on tour as backup for bigger names. Joe loved his mother, but he worshipped his grandmother, who was part Cherokee. His grandmother was the constant light in his young life, and she died before he reached adulthood.

Instead of continuing to Crandall Street from Selleck, Joe turned north toward Court Street, as if we were going to Howie and Margo's. Since I didn't know they had both moved at the end of June, I thought we were going to see Howie, sitting forlorn in his apartment receiving mourners. But when we got out of the car and into the house, Joe passed his door without looking at it and followed instead the sounds of Carol screaming in the next apartment.

I admit to being one of those people who is particularly skeptical of hysteria. I shut right down. Screaming and carrying-on were tools my mother used to get what she wanted or to deflect attention from the rising piles of possessions around us. The result is that it's hard for me to take high drama seriously, so when I saw Carol scrunched up on the floor in the corner of her living room, whose light and air was shut off by curtains, screeching, "He killed her, Joe, he killed her," I didn't really think much of it. First of all, I didn't consider Carol a reliable reporter. Whenever Joe and I crashed on her sofa in the fall of 1975, I couldn't help but notice that she did a lot of crashing too. This was before Howie and Margo moved into the apartment across the hall, and yet we ran into Howie at her place more than any other. I never knew how he knew Carol, just as I didn't know how Joe knew her. How she ever met anyone, I don't know, because it seemed as if she never stepped out of that apartment her entire life. She slept a lot. At first, I used to think she was just a very tired person but eventually figured out it was somewhat more than that. She and Howie often slipped away into her bedroom together, and only Howie came back out. I never looked too closely at the probability that she was shooting up in that room, but when I saw her crying on the floor,

I was quick to attribute it to junk. I had to find something to explain away her crazy talk. Carol had gotten it into her head that Howie killed Margo because she used to hear them fight all the time. She had told us this before. She was telling us again. The walls were cheap and thin. There was a lot of screaming and sounds of furniture crashing.

So what? They were stressful, these interracial relationships. Joe and I fought all the time too. Calm down, Carol. Be cool. After all, Margo liked her hit of acid, and she dabbled in both the occult and drug dealing. Not only could a person get into all sorts of trouble walking down those paths, there was bound to be some exaggerated emotion along the way.

"I'm afraid, Joe." Carol pulled at her long black hair. Strands of it were caught in her fingers and silver rings. "What are we going to do? He's going to kill me too."

I lit up a smoke and sorted through the junk mail on the kitchen table while Joe knelt on one leg next to Carol, talking softly.

Note to younger self: Fear is different from hysteria, dear girl. Fear is real and it has its purpose, helping us to escape from danger or death. You can bet that Carol had good reason to be afraid. It wouldn't have hurt to be a little bit more fearful yourself.

After a while, Joe got Carol to quiet down, saying what, I don't know. I was busy studying the Caldor flyers. As we were leaving, Joe told her: "Lock the door behind us, sugar, and jam it with a chair."

Carol's girls, Debbie and Elizabeth, who seemed to adore her, were not home. They both had after-school jobs at a supermarket and were always working. On Carol's birthday that winter, they had pooled their money and bought her a boxed set of stainless steel flatware. I'm sure they wondered why teaspoons, an essential component of a junkie's kit, kept disappearing from the house. Worse, maybe they didn't wonder. They were so industrious I imagine they are CEO's of major corporations today. They have proved elusive, as has Carol, and I have been unable to track any of them down. The girls might not have had their mother's last name, or even the same fathers, and Carol does not even show up in the 1970s census. Her real name might not have been Sullivan. They seemed to live in a shadow world. I once went grocery shopping for Carol with specific directions to go to Debbie's check-out counter at a certain time, with a long list and a few dollars. She said not to worry about the money, Debbie would work it out. This was back in the day before scanners, and Debbie proceeded to manually register the groceries in at pennies on the dollar or push them past her without keying them in at all. I paid under ten dollars for close to a hundred dollars' worth of food, a huge amount for groceries at the time. I knew there was going to be some slippage, but I didn't know the extent of the scam until it was going on in front of me. I was barely breathing, but I couldn't back out. I was the designated hitter. Carol couldn't do it because as the mom she would be under suspicion, and as I have said, I had never seen her leave the house. Joe couldn't do it because as a black man he was always under suspicion. We were staying on Carol's sofa at the time, so the shopping trip was our rent. When Joe sent me in, he insisted that ripping off the supermarket was not just okay but justifiable because it was a ghetto store that ripped off the black community. The prices were higher than in the white neighborhoods, the quality of the produce lower, the store itself was dirty, and it smelled. "It's not stealing," Joe said, "it's balancing the scales," then waited outside in the car.

As I rolled my mountain of food toward the exit, the white manager came hurrying after me. "Miss." He held out my scarf. It must have slipped off my sweaty head at the counter. "You dropped this," he said, with a smile.

I looked over his shoulder for security guards. I waited a beat, expecting a punch line that never came.

"Thank you," I took my scarf and stuffed it in my coat pocket. I was the only white customer in the store, and when I left, there were none.

The fruit rotted by the next day and filled the apartment with flies.

At any rate, with the girls at work, it meant Joe and I left Carol alone in that apartment, terrified and shaking. Shame on us. I was operating under the delusion that we were humoring her. It's funny to think that all along, I might have been the one being humored. Out in the hall, we could hear scuffing noises with the furniture, then a thud on the other side of the door. Joe tried the latch, was satisfied, and we left. I'm guessing Carol crawled back to her corner. For all I know, she's still there. I never saw her again.

IT WAS DARK by the time we returned home and climbed up the exterior flights of wooden stairs. There were no interior stairs, just that, the rickety fire escape. The door at the top of the stairs was unlocked, as it usually was, seeing as how there was nothing to steal. There was a bolt on the inside, but no key that I knew of. This was July, so it was very stuffy on third floor. No lights were on, which meant that our roommates, Mark and David, weren't home yet. No music was coming from Mrs. Cornaro's apartment downstairs. Joe walked into the apartment ahead of me and switched on the living room light. Howie seemed to roll off the sofa and sit up at the same time.

"They think I did it," he said, rising slightly and staring at Joe. His eyes were unblinking, wide and terrified.

Well, there you have it. If I had for even one moment entertained the idea that Howie had killed Margo, his physical presence in our apartment confirmed that he did not. There he was! On my sofa. I knew him and I did not know murderers. I was young. I believed I knew what I knew.

And yet what did I really know? I didn't know whether he had already been questioned by the police. I didn't know what he and Joe talked about after I left the room, or whether Howie spent the night on that sofa. He could have been asking for advice or begging for help. Maybe he was seeing how his story went over with Joe before he had to face the law, if he hadn't done so already. In the absence of facts, anything was possible. I might have found out some of those facts by asking Joe, but I didn't. I said nothing. I asked nothing.

I had my own problems. We had our own problems. I did not want to hear about dead bodies. Dead bodies could just stay way over there. I was already building a wall between me and Margo's death. I said some comforting words to Howie, how awful it all was. What else was there to say? What was safe to say?

Howie and Joe stayed in the living room, and I excused myself and went to bed. I shut them out. Howie was gone in the morning. For all I knew, the police picked him up at the apartment that night. I slept a lot at that time, and through anything.

O N JULY 20, five days after the mystery body first appeared on the front page, the follow-up, now that Margo was identified, was on page six. "Probe continues in arrow death." What happened to Dead White Woman Fever? Poor Margo was getting pushed farther back in the paper every day. Go away, go away, go away. The police said they were questioning a boyfriend about whom she had complained of assault. A boyfriend. Who else but Howie? The paper knew by now who he was and what color he was. A black man might have killed a Darien woman with a bow and arrow, and they hide the story on page six? It was the sort of story that sold papers. Reading this at the Ferguson, it reinforced my theory that Howie was not seriously a suspect, because he was just mentioned in passing, but it was confusing. Why wasn't this more of a story?

According to Captain O'Connor, Margo herself had no police record, but she had contacted the police on several other occasions in addition to the assault complaint. No charges were ever formally lodged. Carol was right. Margo and Howie had a violent relationship, but I had never suspected. When I was growing up, children were fair game, but beyond TV, I had never seen a man hit his wife, not in my family or in families around me, so I had no eye for domestic violence. Margo's face was often puffy, but I attributed that to chemicals, not fists. Joe and I fought, but never physically. On rare occasions, he restrained me from leaving, which was completely unnecessary since I had nowhere to go.

The short article also said the police were questioning several friends. Joe was one of them. Not that he told me. He told me nothing, so I don't know what they discussed, but they must have talked about the night Howie was on our sofa, because I was interviewed about that as well. I had to call in late for work one day to talk to the police, and the head teller was speechless. The bank did not know I lived with a black man when they hired me, and from the first time he came to pick me up from work, they treated me differently, coolly. They probably ran to my cashbox for a quick audit.

Joe was present while I was questioned, which even at the time seemed odd. It also seemed strange that the interview took place not at the police station downtown but at the nearby Colonnade Restaurant. It could have been that Joe suspected Howie was keeping track of who was going in and out of the station and requested the change of venue. The officer, who was white, didn't even have a notepad and pencil, but since I had no experience in such matters except for what I had seen on TV shows, what did I know? Joe had prepped me, saying that only fools give the police more information than they ask for, no matter what. He told me that all the detective would ask was what had Howie said the night we found him on the sofa in our apartment, and he was right.

It didn't even occur to me to ask Joe how he knew what the detective would ask. I was still thinking Joe was so smart, and this was just more proof of that. At any rate, the officer wasn't very curious. He never asked whether I had ever heard Howie talk about bow and arrows, or whether I ever heard him mention what his weapon of choice would be if he were going to kill someone. Joe stared at me intently the entire time.

After fifteen minutes, before I even finished my cup of coffee, the officer said thank you and I said goodbye. I left for work wondering why I'd even been called in. It was not an interview that would have stirred up any suspicions about Howie.

BACK IN THE LIBRARY basement, I found nothing in the paper for close to a week, then, on July 26, on page six, "Probe continues in Olson slaying, still no suspects":

> Capt. Thomas O'Connor said the investigation has provided information about Miss Olson's whereabouts up to 2:30 am, July 3, on or about the day she is believed to have been fatally shot with a heavy grade bow and arrow, but that the course of events beyond that is still a mystery. Earlier, the captain reported police were questioning friends, including a boyfriend whom she had at least once filed an assault complaint against.

That's the article in its entirety. Why wasn't the paper making a bigger deal about this murder? The editors knew the main suspect was a black drug dealer. Could there have been pressure on the paper from real estate developers to suppress the publication of any story that smacked of a racially charged murder? The mayor? There couldn't be worse publicity for a city that was trying to lure companies out of New York.

Really, the paper was being as tight-lipped as Joe.

There was something else significant about this small mention, something that had not been in the other articles. It said 2:30 a.m. I couldn't figure out whether it was 2:30 the morning of the Fourth of July, or actually on the third, but the time itself led me to believe everyone involved was all messed up. The earlier article had stated that she was staying with Stamford friends. So, she was at a party and left it at 2:30 in the morning. If everyone was tripping or stoned, anything could happen. Maybe even a two-arrow accident.

Another significant point: This was the final article on Margo. I didn't know that as I sat there gazing into the dim gray light of the microfilm projector. I knew from my call to the Stamford police that her case was unsolved, but I still believed that I was going to come across an article naming more suspects or, barring that, an article saying the police had run out of leads and that was that. Something.

But as I continued to scroll through the tapes, holding out hope for resolution, I found nothing more about Margo. Nothing. Her murder was a study in silence. Margo's story, as far as the paper was concerned, had come to an abrupt end with the July 26 story. The next day would have been her twenty-fifth birthday. There was never an obituary in the *Advocate* or the weekly newspaper in Wilton, where her mother lived.* The librarian said that obits were at the discretion of the family and were often omitted "in cases like these." Her death had become a shameful thing. At the end-of-the-year roundup of Stamford events, published in the *Advocate* on New Year's Eve 1976, the article mentioned the discovery of a woman's body, but not her name. They did not even print her name. Margo was killed twice, once by a bow and arrow and then by the paper's whiting her out. The article included the police shooting of Howie, without using his name either. They were erased from history.

---

*There was an obituary in the Darien newspaper, but since the articles never mentioned that she grew up there, I never looked.

The paper certainly seemed to have been doing the public no service by dropping the Margo story so abruptly. Serious crime in Stamford was up sixteen percent in the first six months of 1976 from the same period the year before, which was already pretty high, but murders were still newsworthy events, especially one so "shrouded in mystery." A woman had met a violent and disturbing end within the city limits, and who knew whether she would be the last? Some Robin Hood sicko in tights might have been stalking the streets. Shouldn't the paper—or the police—have issued the usual cautions about taking care against such a possibility?

Perhaps they would have, if they weren't already sure it was Howie. But why not keep up the heat in the paper? Surely, it can't be because the paper lost interest in the story, a gruesome murder of a young white woman. Maybe the police department itself was downplaying it to the reporters. All this silence. It seems just plain strange that the moment Howie was identified as a suspect, the investigation went underground. This fed into my original theory that the police wanted the black man dead for the death of the white woman. They were on a mission, and they didn't care to have an audience reading about their progress.

There. I still had my racism story in my pocket.

This theory still begged the question of who killed Margo, so I continued scrolling through the archives, one eye still looking for Margo and the other looking for Howie. In the same way that I couldn't remember when Margo died, I had no idea when Howie died.

*T*HROUGH THE first half of 1976, Joe picked up small pockets of cash brokering cheap used cars, which was little more than reading the classifieds, finding a buyer in a bar, then taking a cut. Mostly, he borrowed money from friends against the insurance settlement he was still waiting on, from the car accident that had created the scar down the side of his face. At that point, the money was so far off as to mean nothing, and nothing is what his friends got repaid. Before I got the job at the bank, I was bringing in a little coin from the Italian restaurant, and then I got fired for answering the phone incorrectly, apparently an offense worse than spilling soup on laps. When the owner fired me, he said he was sorry, since he admired what I was trying to do.

Really? What was it, exactly, that I was trying to do?

Oh right. Something about equality. That mission seemed a long way back. Right then, all I was trying to do was make rent. When I came back home an hour after leaving the restaurant, Joe shrugged, and we went out to lunch (read: drink) at the Lemon Tree, a restaurant that would figure in the story Howie told the police about where he last saw Margo. But that was later. For now, I was licking my wounds, although losing a job wasn't something to get upset about in Joe's lights. It was what he expected from the world. As long as I got another job soon, who cared? As long as I stayed busy, not just for the money, but because he claimed that bitches who didn't work got depressed. Yes, he actually used the word "bitches," with only the thinnest edge of humor. And no, this theory did not hold true for men. He seemed perfectly content to just hang around our Crandall Street apartment and run up the phone bill.

Some of these calls were to my mother. After months of complete silence, where my parents didn't even know where I was, Georgia, who believed that to dwell on racism was to carve a hole in one's heart, convinced me to call them in March and thaw the relationship. She did not take their disapproval personally. "When people don't like folks they don't even know, it's something in themselves they hate, sugar, not us." It was a short call, just to say I was alive, but it got the lines of communication somewhat open, lines that Joe immediately filled.

Joe saw my mother as a worthy opponent. Being a Scorpio, he insisted he understood her better than I did. He'd tell her jokes to get her to laugh. I remember overhearing this one story: In the town of Demopolis, Alabama, where Georgia was from, her uncle was the undertaker. It was difficult to get payment from families after burial, and the uncle was spending more time chasing after bills than tending to the dead. He became so irritated with the community that he started demanding the money before burial. When the first customer balked, he arranged the corpse on his front porch in a rocking chair. He was paid soon enough, buried the body, and he never had a problem with overdue bills again. Nothing like a dead body lying around to get a point across. I could tell my mother was laughing against her better judgment on the other end of the line, and when her defenses were down like that, he would call her on her shit. Not just her racism, which she denied, saying that they were only worried about how difficult my life would be if I married a black man, he also called her on her materialism, which she did not deny. She loved her stuff and told Joe he was just jealous, which was the truth. He wanted everything she had.

These calls, which in the days before unlimited calling were not cheap, would sometimes last an hour. If I was home, I'd try to put an end to them, but that often backfired and made him pursue his prey even harder. He wanted to win her over or wear her down.

Georgia pressed me to go visit my parents on Easter. "Like Jesus's triumphal entry into Jerusalem" was how she put it. I was tentative but I went. My mother was icy and my father took me aside.

"Tell your friend to stop calling your mother," he said. "It gets her upset."

That's exactly why he calls, I wanted to say, but didn't. "She can just hang up if she doesn't want to talk to him," I said, suspecting that in her own way, she welcomed the calls. They gave her ammunition against him, and us.

"She won't do that," he said, "she doesn't want to lose you."

Lose me? It was a surprising admission, considering she was the one who chased me away and seemed uninterested in any reconciliation. All this took place outside. She did not invite me in the house or offer me anything to eat or drink to prolong my visit. I shrugged. "There's not much I can do about that." Then I got back on my donkey and left.

AT ANY RATE, Joe usually called my mother while I was at work, so I was only vaguely aware of it, or at least until the bill came, which I read carefully to track calls to his old girlfriends across the country. One month, there was a $60 charge on our phone bill for a call to Hawaii. When Joe called Ma Bell to contest it, they took it right off. Their excuse: They thought it might have been ours because we had a history of so many long-distance calls. The telephone company could not have known that Joe was black, but he made the connection to racism anyway. He said it was like the police randomly picking up black men off the street if there had been a crime committed anywhere in the city, just because some black men had been known to commit crimes in the past. This held true for all black men everywhere, even for the elite few who lived north of the Merritt Parkway. The Chambers Brothers, who were friends with Joe and Georgia, owned a house there and were constantly harassed by the police. Jackie Robinson lived in North Stamford and was still alive when Joe was growing up. Robinson was not just a baseball legend, he was a pillar of the community, black and white. As is often the case for children of famous people, life was a mixed blessing for his oldest son, Jackie Jr. He had money and prestige but also some emotional problems, made worse by ostracism in his all-white school, made worse even still by the ridicule he suffered from the parents of his teammates on his Babe Ruth softball team. Shame on them. He put down his glove and left the team.

He enlisted in the army and, like so many others, brought home a heroin addiction from Vietnam. He produced a long Stamford Police rap sheet of drug, guns, and gambling, but cleaned himself up. He died in June 1971 in a car accident on the Merritt, coming home late one night from the rehab that had turned him around. He was twenty-four years old.

According to Joe, who was twenty at the time, Jackie Jr. had been constantly harassed by the local police for being black and rich. An unforgivable combination. Joe and his friends, who emulated Jackie Jr. more than his father, did not cotton to the Stamford *Advocate*'s account of Jackie's accident. They believed that he was killed by the police in a high-speed car chase for DWB, Driving While Black. Does it help that there is overwhelming evidence to show that Jackie Jr. fell asleep at the wheel? No, it does not. In Joe's world there was no such thing as overwhelming evidence to the contrary.

There are no neutral facts. Not when they come filtered through a white police force, a white newspaper, and a white world. The official story might mean many things, but it almost certainly never means the truth. If a black man was dead, you could bet there was a white cop with a grin on his face not too far away.

In Joe's defense, the opposite of a lie might be a truth, but the opposite of a truth might be another truth. That's what I discovered in my time spent in the *Advocate* archives. No outright lies, no outright truths. Just events to be interpreted according to your history.

Early on in Joe's novel, there is a scene of Jackie Jr. in a red Ferrari cruising up Summer Street, passing Joe Louis in front of the Dairy Queen not too far from Court Street. Jackie says hey. Joe says hey back. The next thing Joe knows, cop lights are flashing, and Jackie leaves a trail of smoke as he heads home to North Stamford. After an all-points bulletin based on a falsified report of a stolen Ferrari by Detectives Ligi and Fachetti—the real-life core of Stamford's narcotics squad—the Stamford and state police chase Jackie Jr. into a stone bridge, and he's dead on impact.

> Chalk another dead nigga up for the white man, Joe thought. But Jackie's death was not in vain, if for no other reason than that Joe was determined to never let those bastards do that to him. Joe swore to himself as he read the article that for his whole life he would do what he wanted with whom he wanted and where he wanted, and no one would deter him, ever.

Joe had actually been doing what he wanted to do for a good long time before that. But never mind. Joe the character was determined to get his own way, at any cost, for the rest of his story. Joe and Stamford both. They were so determined. Nothing, no nothing, was going to stand in the city's way in the seduction of New York City corporations. Certainly not an unsavory murder like Margo's. Especially not one located in North Stamford, where realtors stood ready to sell pricey homes to incoming executives who would work at the new corporate park. Stamford could not start looking like New York City, the violent beast the corporations were clawing their way out of. They were not going to relocate near a dead body that reeked of racial complications. No way. We need to get that shit out of sight.

In a July 1976 editorial, a few days after Margo was buried, the paper urged the city to keep itself attractive to corporations. This editorial was called

"Whither Stamford." On first reading, I thought it said, "Whiter Stamford." This editorial came on the heels of Margo's identification, right around the time the police were interviewing Howie. The editor was warning Stamford not to become another New York City, what with its traffic, air pollution, and crime. "It is imperative that the city do everything possible to keep these problems under control."

Everything possible.

A few days later, the police performed a desultory arrest of a gambling ring, nabbing fourteen people. After a bunch of winks, they let each other go. A couple of days after that, the mayor ordered a city probe of extra payments to cops, including to O'Connor, who was heading Margo's investigation. In that same issue, there is a photograph of a black shooting suspect escorted by a phalanx of white police. There was no article to go with the photo, no reference to what the shooting involved, just the photo of Stamford turning whiter by the hour.

*A*FTER MARGO DIED, the summer was quiet. I worked at the bank and Joe did whatever it was Joe did. We did not talk about a wedding, but Joe would sometimes talk about the child we would have someday. It would be a boy, like him, and an only child, like him. To prepare his son to live comfortably in two worlds, instead of being stuck in between them as he felt himself to be, he'd send him to Eton during the school year and to a job in Harlem in the summer.

Eton? You've been mostly living on sofas and floors since college, and you're sending your son to Eton? But at that time, I still saw no discrepancy between how he saw his life and what it really was. And in the end, he was not that much off the mark. His son, Asko, grew up in London. While it might not have been Eton, he had a proper British schooling and the right accent. I have not been able to track him down.

Asko was conceived during a trip Joe made to England to buy a car not too long after we broke up. Why England? Joe was a bit of a snob, which is often not an overblown sense of self but a defense against feelings of inadequacy. The armaments of this defense are the finer things in life, objects that will tell a story about who you are, or who you think they are. In the same way he wanted a royal education for his imaginary son, he wanted to own the car they used as well, the iconic white 1959 Rolls Royce Silver Cloud, the same car my father had once promised to buy for my mother if she'd get her license. Funny, that.

The Asko trip was the second time Joe went to England. The first time was in the spring of 1977, when we were living in Westport, and Joe went there with insurance settlement money in his pocket. He bought a white 1959 Bentley and a kit to convert it to a Rolls. The cars were identical on the surface except for the grill. He shipped both car and kit to the states, where he planned to resell it as a Rolls for a great deal more money. When the car was converted, he drove it from bar to bar and still owned it when I left him. Denise, who stayed behind in our Westport house with her friend Irene, reported that he crashed it a couple of times, then sold it for almost nothing.

Ignoring the fact that the first time he bought and sold an English car was a bust, he went back again late in 1977, just months after I left. He was looking for another car, but he was also trying to track down Stanley Kubrick and pitch him a screenplay he wrote. I can't say whether he found either a car or Kubrick, but he slept with a white German woman while he was there and got her pregnant. A few months later, she came to the states to see what Joe wanted to do about it. He hid. I sometimes wonder whether she got pregnant by that particularly romantic Joe Louis method of throwing birth control pills out a car window. When she came gunning for him, he was already living with a new woman, possibly his hairdresser. Right before I left him, I could not help but notice he was getting his hair cut far too frequently.

Joe refused to man up, but Georgia did. She'd paid for a number of abortions in her time on behalf of Joe, so she would have gladly paid to support a grandchild. She housed the woman and bought her maternity clothes, but when Joe continued to hide out and hold out, the woman left the country in a fury, saying no one, not Joe, not Georgia, was ever going to see that child. Asko, from what I can tell, was born in August 1978, one year after I left Joe.

His mother kept her promise for as long as she had her son under her control. Joe went twice to England, on Georgia's dime, to try to find his son and failed. But at seventeen, Asko tracked down Georgia, who was still at the same address where his own mother had stayed so many years before. Through Georgia, he found his father. At that point, in the mid 90s, Joe was living in Tompkins Square. Susan Mingus told me that after she and Joe broke up, he went through a period of homelessness, even living in a shelter for a while, before attaching himself to a tall, red-headed, very aristocratic-looking woman. He moved into her basement apartment on Tompkins Square, and their relationship lasted a while, but when this woman tired of his drinking, she couldn't get rid of him. Susan said it was like "Bartleby, the Scrivener": Joe preferred not to leave. He dug in, and in the end, like the narrator in Melville's story, the aristocratic woman had to leave her own apartment to be rid of him. There was a patch of dirt out back Joe called his garden, where he would sit and drink his gin, living in his imaginary world, as he had always done. He stayed there until his liver stopped functioning. He did not survive the arrows of his own outrageous fortune.

Ah, Bartleby.

But Joe was still alive when Asko flew over from England, land of Eton. They had a wonderful reunion. I saw a picture of them altogether, Georgia, Joe, and Asko, three generations sharing one face. The young man was handsome, just like his dad, but with slightly lighter skin and straighter hair. They looked so happy. According to Pierre, Asko became a barrister, the lawyer that Joe never got around to being. I wondered whether in that moment Joe had any remorse about his life, if he regretted the decisions he had made. Or, having grown up without a father himself, maybe he felt it had just made his son stronger, even without those summers in Harlem.

I'm glad Joe's son, unlike Joe himself, was able to track his father down in time. A few years later, and he would have just missed him. Asko, having fulfilled the important developmental step of facing his father, returned to London and started his life, which included a son of his own. Georgia helped him get dual citizenship and a U.S. passport, then she got a postcard from him in India, then one from Brazil. He did not come back to the States for Joe's funeral and could not be found to let him know about Georgia's.

IN THE SUMMER OF 1976, Joe and I worked sporadically on his state assembly campaign, for which he was a perpetual candidate every two years since running for mayor in 1971. (Slogan for 1974: "Watergate Means Change.") State representative was a job that had a token salary and was not full time, but it came with access to the kind of privileged information concerning state and city contracts and real estate development that can make ordinary people wealthy, fast. I thought it was a legislative body with the capacity to enact social justice. What can I say? It was a job, like that of mayor, in which Joe felt he would not have to answer to the Man. In a newspaper article, he was quoted as saying, "One reason I'm running is that I'm unemployed and I'd love a job," so on that and a platform dedicated to legalizing marijuana—neither of which I knew at the time—he collected contributions from his rich white friends from Cherry Lawn. I helped on the campaign after work and on weekends, canvassing door to door in the South End, while he campaigned in local bars. It was the neighborhood where we had driven through the block party the year before, where I met Howie. One afternoon, while canvassing, I passed a shirtless black man in camouflage pants walking down the street with a military rifle slung over his shoulder. He kept his head down, muttering. Good god, a crazy 'Nam vet with a weapon! I was on the other side of the street, alarmed, but not particularly frightened. I was wrapped in a cloth of privilege and political righteousness and nothing could harm me.

Ha, ha, ha. You go, girl.

I smiled, perhaps insanely, as we passed each other. He didn't seem to know I existed. He was wrapped in his own wretched battle and could not escape.

"As long as it's not hidden, it's legal" was all Joe had to say about the gun, then asked how many votes I'd collected. Considering the historically lax voting habits of drunks and sociopaths, we'd collected just about none. Joe, who managed to get his name on the ballot by petition, barely even showed in the primary. I'm not sure he even had his own vote. He had fallen off the rolls and had failed to register at Crandall Street. If he managed to vote that day, it was not with me.

IT WAS NOT JOE'S ONLY campaign that summer. In his ongoing crusade to make me see life through his eyes, we would argue about America. Even when he was trying to be romantic, like taking me out to dinner after picking up some cash at a card game or brokering a used car, he would not let up. One night, we went to a restaurant that was nice enough to have frog legs on the menu, because that is what I ordered. Joe had a scotch. He had a few of them and then began to attack my upbringing, as if I were a symbolic stand-in for white America, representing an entire race for past crimes. He did so calmly, without anger or spite, as if he were standing in front of a blackboard pointing at convoluted diagrams of my racial history. In Susan Mingus's 2002 memoir of her life with Charles, *Tonight at Noon,* she wrote about their own ongoing conflict about race and female autonomy, and his calm accusation, "You're so American." American has always meant white, with no slack cut for being a white woman. As much as some of us might have wished, we couldn't remove ourselves from the dominant culture, pretending our own hands were clean. We'd reaped the benefits of both a slave economy and a cheap labor pool. We'd done nothing to keep the dogs from being set on the crowds, and we were there at the lynchings. We baked the pies for the picnics afterward. It is a troubling heritage to bring to a relationship. This wasn't about guilt, Joe insisted. It was about getting to the truth and acknowledging it, or else society would never change.

But the truth hurt. I stared at my untouched dinner of amphibious legs, teeny webbed limbs arranged on a plate, as he continued to lecture me on what today we would call my white privilege,* and what he called my racial entitlement and advantages. Better access to housing, schools, and jobs. But what if I hadn't asked for those advantages? I wanted to pack up slavery and Jim Crow and put it in a box marked "Ancient History." I wanted us to start with a clean slate, two people in love, whose hearts were indifferent to the color of our skin. But arguing about my own nonracism was missing the point. I was trying to insist we were equal, when he was intent on emphasizing our difference. Our American experiences could not be compared. The Irish were discriminated against when they got here but assimilated in time. Blacks were brought here against their will and enslaved by the white elite and continued to suffer oppression on a daily basis. I had to understand that to understand him. I had to own it. This is what my culture did.

Agreed. There was no question that the plight of the middle-class white girl in a white male hegemony paled in comparison to that of black men and women (who had to bear the pressures of both racism and sexism) in their historical struggle for even the most basic rights. But I suggested to Joe that we might sometimes be united in our disenfranchisement, citing Shulamith Firestone in *The Dialectic of Sex,* as well as John and Yoko's 1972 song, "Woman Is the Nigger of the World." When I pointed out that the subjugation of women predated institutional race-based slavery, Joe said I didn't know shit about inequality and prejudice, that there was no comparison. White women didn't know from repression. And now, with feminism, in bad economic times, they were after the limited share of benefits white men were just beginning to grant nonwhites.

In a snit, I told him that men of any color were so entitled they confused their wants with their needs, and he more than anyone else. We left in a huff, with me in tears and my frog legs barely touched. Just as well. I had only liked the idea of them anyway, more curious than anything, not thinking they'd actually look like legs and taste like swamp.

*A term that began to be used mostly in academia in the 1980s, but not in general use until the Black Lives Matter movement in the 2010s.

When I read his novel, years later, I found that Joe acknowledged more common ground than he would admit to me. In a section of "Hell at the Apostle's Gate," he's about to make his run for mayor, and his friends advise him to start dating black women.

> "Well, I'll tell you one problem that you're going to have with the black vote," Danny began knowingly. "It's the perception that you're a little on the white side. I heard some of the sisters quietly saying how you're always with some fay* broad all the time."
> "Well actually," Joe began, a bit caught off guard, "I do dig white women, but more importantly they dig me. And really the white man has dogged the white woman almost as much as the black man."

Joe told me that he had gone on a date with a sister for the sake of his campaign, and she ordered two sandwiches and packed one up in her pocketbook to bring home. He loved her chutzpah, but he was used to women taking care of him, not the other way around. Buying into the gender racist myth of the black woman as strong and the white woman meek, he wrote in his novel that black women were on to his game, the implication being that they would not have tolerated for one moment what I put up with. But I doubt that. Joe was a pretty charming devil. In another part of the novel, he wrote, "He could hear the voices of his uncles telling him 'black women would see through your jive and waste your black ass for your bullshit.'" Whatever reasons Joe had for dating only white women, he laid the cause of his defection on black women. For all his insistence that I acknowledge his culture and racial history, he seemed to be ignoring half of it.

ALL IN ALL, going out to dinner was no relaxing break in our lives, but I rarely said no. It was something to do. Looking back on that summer, I realize now that we rarely socialized, that we never went together to visit all those friends who had opened their homes and sofas to us the fall before, like Carol, Ronny and Leila, and others. I never saw anyone with whom Margo's death might become a topic of conversation. Joe did, but I didn't. I was kept in a bubble of silence. I don't even remember seeing Georgia during

*"Fay," short for "ofay," is outdated slang for a white person.

that time, and if I did, I know we never spoke Margo's name. So other than work, there was just the occasional dinner out. Ten weeks after Margo died, Joe and I went to the Marriott with the revolving restaurant at the top. The dining room was mostly windows, so diners could enjoy the expansive views of Long Island Sound and, on clear days, the New York City skyline without having to look at the bulldozed squalor at the hotel's feet, where the old city once stood. It was Joe's idea to go there, and an odd one. It was cheesy, expensive, and not known for its food at any price.

On the way up to the restaurant, the elevator stopped after just a few floors and Howie walked in. My memory was that I hadn't seen him since he was on my sofa the night Margo's body was identified, but according to Joe, I had. In a box of Joe's personal papers I got from Pierre after Georgia's death in 2014, I found three handwritten pages that never made it into the typed manuscript of his novel. In this scene, Howie comes to our apartment later in the summer of Margo's murder, arriving as we are on our way out to jai alai* with some black guy named Josie, whom I do not remember, but Joe called him "one of the roughest and toughest dudes in town."

"Joe had not seen Howie for some time and had been sort of dodging him since Howie had become the prime suspect in the apparent murder of Margo, his spacey girlfriend. . . . In his heart Joe knew that Howie would never kill Margo, not even in anger or rage." Joe goes on to discuss the possibility of cult connections, and maybe her murder was a Satanic ritual. Having said that, Joe waffles. "If Howie did not kill her, he probably knew who did; especially since he was always with her." Then he goes on to describe how Howie had crashed into the bicentennial cake in front of the police station. "The detective handling the case, Ed McNulty, who was an old friend of Joe's, had joked to Howie that he had indeed wanted to see and question Howie but that his entrance was a bit dramatic and extreme. This accident seemed to cast a suspicious pall upon Howie, even to his friends. . . . Joe was unpleasantly surprised to see him." After some chitchat, Joe asks, "'So Zow did you straighten out everything with McNulty?'

"'What's to straighten out. I told him I don't know anything about Margo and what happened to her,' Howie stated nervously.

"'Well I went in to see Ed and he asked me if I thought you did it. I told

*A Basque sport that had just opened in Bridgeport, a gambling alternative to horse or dog racing.

him no I didn't and that what I knew of Margo that she was into some weird ass shit and weird ass friends and that anything was possible,' Joe said.

"'Yea, that's right. You said right. So where you guys off to?' Howie asked."

Joe tells Howie that we are going to jai alai, and that Josie doesn't want him to come along.

"Well I can go where I want," said Howie, who began flicking the seven-inch blade and looking ominously at Josie to show that he was not scared of him and he was his equal. Josie looked ominously over at Howie. Josie looked like what he was, which was a tough and danger-ous man. "So Josie you got a problem with that?" Howie said as he continued stroking his blade and starting to become fearful. Josie took his hands out his pockets and crossed them, smiled for a brief moment and just stood there. Howie's fumbling with the knife had caused him to cut himself. "Yo don't bleed on my couch nigger," said Joe, as JoeAnn went to get a paper towel.

The altercation ends after I, the JoeAnn in the novel, calmly return and hand Howie a paper towel to stop the bleeding. Joe hustles Howie offstage, and after I dab at a few drops of blood on the sofa, we go to jai alai. Out on the street, after we have watched Howie drive off, Joe, according to his ac-count, turned to Josie and said, "'Thanks for not wasting my homey. I think he's lost it. He's not right. Besides who the hell wants to clean up all that blood there'd be?'

"'Not me,' said JoeAnn. Josie and Joe began to laugh loudly."

Just another day on Crandall Street. I don't remember this scene, al-though it does sound like something well worth being blocked out, what with that murder suspect in my apartment, a knife in his hand, and the bad-ass Josie. Not to mention the blood. Who knows whether it really happened? The point is, Joe used the event to express his ambiguous opinion on Howie's guilt. He writes this all down in the 90s, then decides, for whatever reason, no. He pulls the three pages from the manuscript. The less said, the better. Joe was still afraid of Margo's death and Howie's fate, two decades after the fact. What was he so afraid of?

Back to the night at the Marriott in the elevator. Howie was wearing a blue denim jumpsuit (oh, those 70s fashions), and this time it was Howie who seemed unpleasantly surprised to see Joe, who gave him a wide smirk.

As the door closed behind Howie, he pressed all the elevator buttons, saying something about wanting to go down, not up, then got off on the next floor.

"He was packing heat," said Joe, after he was gone, and we resumed our ascension to the top. He gazed up at the changing floor numbers. "He just bought a gun from the guy who sells them from a room here."

Joe used to say a lot of crazy things to get a rise out of me. If I responded at all, I just said "Huh."

We had a drink at the restaurant and left without dinner. Joe was in a hurry to get somewhere, but wherever it was didn't include me. I went home and he went out.

I THOUGHT I KNEW what I was looking for in the archives when it came to Howie. I believed my memory was quite clear. As I remembered the photo on the front page of the September 29 *Advocate*, Howie was wearing the same jumpsuit I'd seen him in at the Marriott. It was a big picture, big headlines. I could still see the scene, the way Howie was slumped with his head leaning up against the counter in the liquor store, his whole chest a dark, bloody crater. Either he had stood still long enough for one cop to shoot over and over or the whole force aimed and shot at once.

Except that it turned out there was no such image. The real photo surprised me when it showed up on the Ferguson Library screen. He was not in the liquor store but face down in the mud, over by the river, practically next to the Stamford *Advocate* building. He was not in the denim jumpsuit but in jeans and a shirt, which was pulled up as an EMT inspects the wound in the upper left part of his back, right where his heart would be. I was so surprised to see the photo, I thought there had to be another newspaper, a weekly perhaps, so certain I was about my memory of him on the floor. But the librarian assured me that there was no other newspaper. And how could there be a photo of him dying in two separate places anyway?

In Joe's novel, there had been the brief scene of Howie and Margo in the midst of a discussion about cults, then they both disappeared. About a hundred pages later, Howie returns to the page without Margo, but with the law hot on his ass. No reason is given, no explanation offered as to why. "If they're going to treat me like a desperado, I'm going to act like one," he said, and headed to the liquor store with a .357 magnum.

Stamford *Advocate*, Wednesday, 9/29/76, Holdup suspect is killed; cop wounded in gunfight

A robbery suspect is dead and a special police officer was wounded this morning following a holdup at a liquor store on Washington Blvd. in Stamford's South End.

Angris McKeithen, 67, 338 West Ave., a special police officer for more than 25 years, allegedly was shot at point blank range by Howard Carter, 28, 150 Shadow Ridge Rd., after halting Carter on Clinton Ave. following a holdup at the Tower Liquor Store, 902 Washington Blvd. Police said.

Officer McKeithen then emptied his revolver at the fleeing gunman who ran several blocks, but was captured after he was found hiding in bushes near Mill River during a quickly organized police search. Carter, who was shot once, died at 4 a.m.

The actions of the special officer, which won praise this morning from police officials and Mayor Louis A. Clapes, were not the only heroics in the incident, however, as another suspect, Albert A. Steele, was captured after a struggle by a liquor store employee, Alfred Reyes, 38, of 25 Taylor St.

Steele, who has been charged with robbery and assault in the first degree, is being held on $25,000 bond. He was captured and held at gunpoint by Mr. Reyes until police arrived, Stamford Police said.

In reconstructing events surrounding the holdup and double shooting at a press conference this morning, Lt. John Considine, acting detective chief, said police were notified at approximately 8:05 p.m. by a silent alarm at the store.

A few minutes earlier, Lt. Considine said, Carter and Steele allegedly entered the liquor store and confronted Marjorie Kohut, 49, 304 Alfred St., a bookkeeper, who was standing behind the store counter.

Carter, reportedly wearing wig and false mustache, pulled a large .38 caliber weapon while Steele, wearing a ski mask, collected an undetermined amount of cash from the register.

When the robbery suspects entered the premises, however, Mr. Reyes was working in a crouched position in the rear of the store and was not seen by the robbers.

Mr. Reyes reportedly waited until Carter placed the revolver in his belt and moved with Steele toward the front of the store. Mr. Reyes then emerged from behind some merchandise boxes holding his own .38 caliber revolver, and told the two men to halt.

Police alleged that Carter bolted from the store but Steele and Mr. Reyes struggled as the robbery suspect attempted to grasp the pistol from Mr. Reyes. Mr. Reyes overpowered Steele police said, and held him until patrolmen answering the silent alarm arrived at the scene.

Only a few minutes after receiving the alarm call, Special Officer McKeithen called police from a call box on Washington Blvd. and Clinton Ave. and said "I've been shot, I've been shot."

Lt. Considine said police were unsure how Officer McKeithen learned of the robbery but speculated that the special officer may have heard the news over a police radio in his car. Mr. McKeithen was on duty guarding a new elderly housing site on Clinton Ave. at the time.

Mr. McKeithen apparently saw Carter fleeing the scene and halted him on Clinton Ave. Police quoted the special officer as saying Carter allegedly pulled his pistol and shot him in the chest at point blank range. Although badly wounded and bleeding profusely, Mr. McKeithen pulled his own weapon and shot the gunman, police said. He then made his way to the call box on Washington Blvd. and Clinton Ave. where he made his call for help.

Meanwhile, Carter fled the scene and hid in bushes near Mill River.

Responding to the call, Ptlm. Douglas Baker and George Scarano found a witness police said had seen Carter fleeing the scene.

Under the direction of Capt. John Moriarity and Lt. Richard D'Agosstino, police hastily organized a search of the area. At this point, Ptl. Patrick Murphy stopped his patrol car on the opposite side of the river from where Carter was hiding, police said.

The patrolman heard noises in the bushes, waded across the river and apprehended Carter, according to police.

Mayor Clapes commended police for their work and singled out Mr. McKeithen for praise.

The Stamford Police Association, Lt. Considine said, also commended Mr. McKeithen for his devotion and dedication beyond the call of duty.

The front page of the paper looks like an old silent film poster, with the downed villain, Howie, on the left side, and the smiling hero on the right, a studio portrait of McKeithen, a smiling, balding sixty-seven-year-old black man.
A black cop. And there went my story again.
Like the Columbia University student uprising, where white cops stormed the white students and black cops stormed the black students, it seemed care had been taken that the report of Howie's death was presented as black on black. An amazing feat, that, considering there were few fully accredited black cops in Stamford at the time. Angris McKeithen, a World War II veteran and former marine sergeant, was a special police officer* who happened to be in the right place at the right time when Howie robbed the liquor store. He was supposed to be on duty a few blocks away, watching over the elderly.

*Special officers were appointed to two-year terms by the police association. This designation seems to have been mostly reserved for black officers, who were poorly represented on the regular force, and is no longer in use.

Writing about Howie's killing in his novel, Joe claims that Angris, whom he calls Angus, was "disgusting and nefarious" and that he'd done many terrible things in his career. Angris's official record seems pure, but maybe that's what Joe meant. The white man's tools play by the white man's rules. It might have been coincidence that Angris was outside the liquor store when Howie came out, or not. Maybe Angris had gotten a tip that the robbery was going to happen. Stamford was a small world. Lacking evidence for Margo's murder, it might have been a sting organized by the police to get Howie behind bars. Or it might have been a sting to get him killed.

There is much to ponder in this holdup article, which seems to be a carefully crafted rendition of what was read or handed out at the police press conference, a story designed to keep things cool and at arm's length. There are no quotes from witnesses or any of the people in the liquor store or on the street. Except for Howie's age and his parents' address (he had his own address, if not two, so I'm not sure why they used that one), there was nothing about the "gunman"—who he was, what he did for a living, whether he was a native of Stamford, or what. Nor did the article mention that he was a suspect in that summer's recent bow-and-arrow murder. It might have been a small relief to the citizens to know that. Yet much is made of the weaponry. Joe's novel calls Howie's gun a .357 magnum, presumably the one bought at the Marriott, and the *Advocate* article called it a .38 caliber, but they are basically the same gun, the same make that Mr. Reyes had in the liquor store, the same make that McKeithen used on Howie. Standard police issue.

———————

IN THE REAL PHOTO of Howie in the paper, not the one in my memory, his young black body is face down, shirtless, eyes closed, and mouth open. He was no longer wearing the wig and fake mustache mentioned in the article. I wonder whether Joe knew where he got those too, along with the gun. Maybe people who sell guns from hotel rooms also sell disguises in a package deal. Howie was still alive when the photo was taken. The caption said he was being assisted by several officers. Funny word "assisted."

It is at this moment in Joe's novel, with Howie lying on the ground, dying, that we hear these words from his lips: "I just have to get in touch with Joe. Everything will be okay."

Get out of his head, Joe! Let the man have his own final thoughts. Let him call out for his momma. Let him repent his sins. *Let him tell us about Margo.*

Instead, Howie wishes his old buddy, Joe, was there to save the day.

Why is Howie thinking of Joe as he bled out on the bank of the Mill River?

Hey Joe, where you goin' with that gun in your hand? as Jimmy Hendrix used to say.

Joe knew why Howie was at the Marriott. The timing of the holdup meant that Howie went almost directly from the Marriott to the liquor store, a matter of a couple of hours. Time to change his clothes and put on a wig, then meet up with Steele. If Joe wasn't an active participant, he was certainly on the inside, friendly as he claims he was with McNulty. Friendly as he was with Howie.

But the inside of what?

Those of you who know the history of Stamford's police department in the 70s know where this story is going.

JOE AND HIS FRIENDS put on their shades and remained stony-faced and quietly drunk for days. The word on the street, which I had gathered from fragments Joe told me and the muted whispers of our friends, was that the police believed Howie had killed Margo but didn't have the evidence against him, so they killed him. This was the story I carried with me for decades, the story where I assumed that Howie was innocent. But no one was actually saying that. They left that part blank for me to fill in. No one mentioned that the cop who pulled the trigger was black either. Again, I filled in that blank with a white cop.

Guilty or not, Howie must have been desperate to get out of town and away from police questions for a while. A wad of cash would help facilitate that move, but the liquor store was no easy hit. In fact, it was the worst possible hit. Not only that, but Howie had no history of armed robbery. None. It must have been someone else's idea because he knew better. The Tower Liquor Store was almost certainly owned and staffed all by whites, perhaps friends or associates of its builder, Mr. Rich, as were all the businesses that rimmed the bottom of St. John's Towers. Joe and I would grab a slice once in a while from the pizza joint in the building, and the white owner was openly hostile to us. Why'd we go? It was there. We stayed at Ronny and Leila's in the Tower often enough. At any rate, those stores would have been heavily alarmed and armed. The liquor store was close to the highway, but back then, not a straight or easy getaway. As stated in the article, the employee had a gun on him at the time, and probably at all times, even as he stocked the shelves, crouching low behind the merchandise.

On top of everything else, the police were going in and out of the Towers constantly, of which Howie was well aware. Howie was not stupid, so there must have been some compelling reason why he chose a place so familiar, so likely to be on the lookout for someone like him. But he did. Whoever convinced him that this would be a good place to rob was probably the same person who knew that the middle-aged female bookkeeper would be counting out the day's drawer at 8 o'clock at night. Someone told him where to buy the gun, and he must have agreed to be paired with an accomplice, Albert A. Steele, who seems to have been shuffled quickly offstage. (Steele, as in Steal. Who could make this stuff up?) He was the only one in the article who was given no age or address, only that he was held on bail. The story was never followed up, and I have been unable to find him, so I don't know whether he went to jail or was just sent on his way, counting a few bills tucked in his pocket.

––––––––––––––––––––

THE DAY AFTER the robbery article, there was a short piece on the obituary page, "Funeral Saturday for robbery suspect." It stated that Howie had been a lifelong resident of the city and that he was a self-employed jewelry salesman.

Joe wouldn't let me go to Howie's funeral or to the collation at Howie's parents' house afterward. Possibly it was for my own safety, since the underlying premise of Howie's story was that his death, even though it was at the hands of a black officer—who either was the white man's tool or was set up as much as Howie or was just doing his job—was the fault of some fucked-up white chick who got herself killed. It was their worst fear come true about interracial couples. If anything happened to the white woman, the black man would pay the price. The whole black community would pay. They wanted me out of sight. After the funeral, there was not another word about Howie, and things became as quiet as they were after Margo's death. Self-protection kept me from absorbing the enormity of it, and instinct told me not to stare. As with Margo, Joe and I never mentioned Howie again. We whited them out.

*A*LIVE, Howie and Margo held a distorted mirror up to the relationship I was in with Joe. Dead, they got buried, and we moved out of town. We did not discuss this sudden relocation. Joe announced he was sick of Stamford, quite possibly because he had just lost the race for state assembly for the third time, and it had sunk in that he had no political future in that town. He had just gotten his insurance settlement, which made the move possible, but I think the impetus had more to do with Howie's death than lost elections and wherewithal. I transferred to a Mechanics & Farmers branch in Trumbull, and we left for affluent Westport farther up the Connecticut coast on October 1. It was just weeks after Margo's body had been found, and days after Howie was killed by the police. It seemed as if we were being lifted up out of that city by outside forces and deposited elsewhere. We left it all behind. I never saw any of the people we knew there again. I never got to say goodbye to Ronny and Leila or Carol and her girls. I never had a chance to discuss Margo and Howie's deaths with them—or anyone.

The small cities along the coast in Connecticut are suctioned onto I-95 like barnacles on a rope attached to the mother ship, New York. Westport, at over forty-five miles from Grand Central Station, was at that time considered the outermost post that could be considered commutable. The term "exurbia" was coined with it in mind. But as a rule, when people escaped from New York to Westport, it was not with the notion of commuting every day. Residents were usually actors, artists, writers, musicians, and other independently or creatively employed people who needed to be near but not dependent on the city. In *I Love Lucy*, when Desi and Lucy moved out of the city, they moved to Westport. It was an oasis for mixed couples of all sorts, even then. Joe and I jumped from disdained to darlings just by moving ten miles east.

In our wake, the cogs of the Stamford justice machine started creaking, only I was completely unaware of it. It wasn't until years later, at the Ferguson, staring at the screen, scrolling the microfilm past Howie's obituary looking for a follow-up article of any sort, hoping for something more on Margo's murder, that their story developed not so much sense as context.

By now the Ferguson Library archives had been moved to a modern room upstairs, in a more brightly lit and open space, not as private as before, but no longer oppressive. At first, I found periodic follow-ups on the condition of Special Officer McKeithen, with an award night planned for later in the year. An article about the event featured a picture of him smiling, with his arm in a sling. But there was nothing more about Howie, and the investigation of Margo's murder had stopped long before. I put in a new canister, dated October 22, 1976, three weeks after Howie was killed. There had been nothing on him or Margo in any of the cannisters in between. As soon as I got the film focused and saw the headlines, I gasped so loudly that the librarian looked up from her desk.

The upper right headline read, "Kinsella steps down as Chief of Police," and to the lower left, "Low morale, racket ties plague Stamford police." It was the article that framed Howie and Margo's story in one sad, sorry box, and I was sent back to square one.

IN OCTOBER 1976, there were three legs of Stamford: dirty politics, municipal and police corruption, and Anthony Dolan of the *Advocate*. As far as I know, he was not the author of any of the articles on Margo, but he crafted the one on Howie's holdup and death. Dolan grew up in Fairfield and was educated at Yale. He won the 1978 Pulitzer Prize in local investigative specialized reporting his two-year series about Stamford corruption, starting with the October 22 article, six dozen stories in all revealing the many ways that organized crime had infiltrated not just the Stamford Police Department but politicians, firefighters, employees of the department of public works, building, engineering, zoning departments, the board of education, state officials, and the justice system itself. His first breakthrough was the discovery of rigged civil service exams—meaning, the exams needed to join the post office and the fire and police departments. His reporting underscores the importance of a free press in a democracy. What else do we have to expose and investigate corruption and to maintain an informed citizenry? When all levels of the government and justice system are abusing power, where can people go with claims of that abuse? Only the press.

Dolan had been collecting information from anonymous phone calls from good cops on the force for more than a year before the series began. It takes a lot for a cop to drop a dime on a brother. It is not taken lightly in any situation, and in this case they were risking not just their careers but their lives. If not for these brave men (there were no female officers that I know of), Dolan would have had nothing. Because Dolan's informants were anonymous, there was a disclaimer at the beginning of the first article, stating that "the series was prepared several weeks ago and held for extensive rechecking of all facts to assure the accuracy of the details," and that the newspaper was handing over the material to the FBI. It was during this time—in between writing the article and releasing it—that Howie was killed. It was as if the whole city was waiting for Howie to die before sending in the clean-up crew.

The October 22 article forced the resignation of Police Chief Kinsella, who, as I have said, had never been a cop in the first place, having been directly promoted from the post office. There is a photograph of Kinsella shaking the mayor's hand and looking at the camera as if he had a gun to his head, his mouth open, in shock. Whatever Kinsella's role was in the corruption, the mob and the Stamford police were more or less one and the same at that point. Like the desperados and thieves of the Wild West who were the opportunistic scum who came to town ahead of the advancing horde of European immigrants in the nineteenth century, the Gambino family out of New York City had arrived in Stamford one step ahead of the corporations. They were there to scope out the real estate and other money-making enterprises, legal and otherwise, getting ready to open wide for the influx of money that was on its way. When taking over a territory, the first item on the agenda, as any desperado will tell you, is to get the law on your side. Better yet, shoot the sheriff and replace him with one of your own, someone who knows nothing about police work, someone, oh say, from the post office. In gratitude, this person will look the other way, and he will hire whoever he's told to. The Gambinos were the law, calling all the shots.

I thought back to the stories I had been reading in the archives all along, many suggesting mob ties, but the paper was only quoting civic and religious leaders, with no backing from the city. Sometimes they published oblique hints, such as a front-page photo in March 1976 of a body's being dragged from Stamford Harbor. There was no accompanying article. No mention of how this man might have gotten himself in deep water. Nothing. Just a cryptic caption that said who he was, a local man with an Italian name. Either it was a newspaper that didn't ask many questions, or it didn't need to be spelled out. Dolan was now spelling it out, and he did so at great personal risk, with death threats and smashed windshields. It's a wonder he didn't find a horse's head in his bed. But young, white, Yale-educated Dolan felt righteously protected by the First Amendment, perhaps innocently so, and he never blinked. It was his first newspaper job, a career that had been encouraged by William Buckley back at Yale.

Reading Dolan's articles, I learned that it was the Democratic machine, from the city bottom to the state level, that had fostered the corruption. When Joe threw his support to the Republican candidate during his run for mayor, it was to the party who was trying to clean up the mess, even though that mayor, Wilensky, was not successful, and he did not last. Nor did the next one, Frederick Lenz,* a Democrat, who promoted his brother, Eddie, from police sergeant to major while in office. There is no rank of major. It was not until Republican Louis Clapes was elected in 1975 that things began to change. Joe might have done the right thing for the wrong reason, but he was not blinded by party loyalty. He had no trust in any party or for that matter, in American government, in which laws by the white elites have always been used to enslave and oppress people of color for monetary gain.

Whatever Dolan's political leanings were when he started his work at the *Advocate*,** he was a conservative Republican by the time he left. He became Ronald Reagan's main speechwriter, then went on to write for Donald Rumsfeld and Paul Wolfowitz. He worked for Ted Cruz in his 2016 presidential bid and, at the time of this writing, works in Trump's White House. But it was during Dolan's long tenure with Reagan that he coined the term "evil empire." He probably first came up with the phrase while writing about Stamford—but about the Gambinos, not the Russians.

---

*Father of Frederick Lenz III, better known as Rama, Buddhist teacher and purported cult leader.

**His brother, Terry Dolan, was cofounder and chairman of the National Conservative Political Action Committee (NCPAC). He died of AIDS in 1986.

Mystery shrouds finding of body

By THOMAS F. SWEENEY
Advocate Staff Reporter

The partially decomposed body of an unidentified woman, whom police say may be the victim of a homicide, was discovered late Wednesday morning lying in a shallow grave in an overgrown field near the Stamford branch of the University of Connecticut.

Capt. Thomas O'Connor said this morning that there were no visible signs of foul play either on the body or near the grave. But he described the situation as being "definitely a suspicious death, and we are investigating the possibility of homicide."

The State's Chief Medical Examiner, Elliot M. Gross, M.D., was scheduled to perform an autopsy this morning to determine the cause of death and the woman's identity.

Police are reviewing a list of missing persons that contains the names of six Stamford area women who fit the general description of the discovered body.

What began as an exploration of historical gravestones at the old potter's field off Scofieldtown Rd. ended in the nightmarish discovery for Patrick White, a teacher at Stamford High School.

Mr. White had taken his mother and a female cousin to the field around 11 a.m. to show them old grave markers he had seen when formerly employed at the nearby Arboretum. The three reportedly smelled "something foul" as they traversed the lot. When Mr. White ventured into the thicket towards the stench he saw what appeared to be a human arm and a foot jutting out of the ground.

"We were reasonably sure of what we saw but we didn't want to believe it. It was horrible — horrible," recalled Mrs. Martin Mulkerin, Mr. White's cousin. "We were aware of the putrid odor of decay but, knowing the grounds, we thought it must have been a dead animal. Then we saw the newly turned earth — and the arm," said Mrs. William White, Mr. White's mother.

According to Police Capt. Thomas O'Connor, who is heading the investigation, the body was of a woman with strawberry blond hair who was about five feet eight inches tall. It was clothed in blue jeans, a blue and white blouse and a single black, cloth sandal.

Stamford Medical Examiner Sedat Ozcomert, M.D., who appeared at the scene but did not stay until the body was exhumed, said he figured the woman had been dead for one to two weeks. Dr. Gross could not be reached for comment.

Capt. O'Connor said police and medical officials were unable to determine the age of the dead woman at the scene because her face was badly decomposed. He said, however, there were no signs of a struggle.

The detective theorized that an animal had exposed the limbs of the body while digging at the makeshift grave.

Capt. O'Connor said the City owns the field and used to bury its poor there years ago. He said few people knew of the spot and he ruled out the possibility that the woman had been officially

(Continued on Page 2)

FIGURE 1. (*Top*) The first article in the Stamford *Advocate* about finding the body, July 15, 1976.

FIGURE 2. (*Bottom left*) Joe Louis, playing cards, 1976.

FIGURE 3. (*Bottom right*) Author, JoeAnn Hart, 1974. Pleasantville High School photo, taken to include with college applications. Copyright Davis Studios.

AS I READ DOLAN'S first article in the series, my story started bleeding out, again. Joe was right, the police wanted Howie dead, but not in the way he had led me to believe. Howie's death was not so much racism as mob politics. "Declining morale, cover-ups of suspected police crimes including drug pushing, and strong ties between policemen and a racketeer who is closely linked to organized crime are problems that currently plague the Stamford Police Department, an *Advocate* investigation shows." If, in fact, Howie was set up to be killed, it was probably not because he had been living with a white woman who subsequently died under incriminating circumstances, but because, if he'd been arrested or charged with Margo's murder, guilty or not, he would have taken half the police force down with him on the witness stand. He might even have been reckless enough to say as much during his questioning, something to the tune of "You can't touch me."

Was that my story? Perhaps. But it only answered part of it. The fact that the city was run by the Gambinos certainly shed some light on why Howie was dead, but it did nothing to answer the question of who killed Margo. It wasn't looking very good for Howie, but I was still holding out for some other answer. If it was him, I wanted to know. If it wasn't, then who? Most of all, I was still trying to find Margo herself, the person, not the faceless woman at the center of it all.

PART 2

We are adhering to life now
with our last muscle—the heart.

—Djuna Barnes

FOR A LONG WHILE, every time I came across the Stamford file in my computer, it seemed to glow like a black light poster, as if waiting to reach its half-life to become safe to touch. Sometimes I'd open a document called "Stamford, asst" and record a random thought, or I would go on a spontaneous foray on the internet, using key words like "70s Stamford" or "Stamford corruption." Nothing gave me what I wanted, which was to give meaning to what I had, but what I had was not enough. A few newspaper articles, fuzzy memories, and a mountain of unanswered questions. I didn't want to write the story where the black guy killed his girlfriend. That was not my mission, but to find Margo I would have to take the risk of finding out that her murderer really was Howie, someone I knew. Worse, I would have to take the risk that it was not him but someone, known or unknown, who killed Margo for being with a black man. And there was still a chance it was random killer, who put all women at risk.

I did what Joe would do and said fuck it. Even though he didn't want to go near Margo's death with a ten-foot pole, he would have encouraged me to write what I wanted, write what I needed. Write what has to be told.

Who says that I didn't learn anything from Joe? I just don't give him enough credit.

Wait, then I read what he wrote about me in his novel: "He knew she had gone through a plethora of changes since she had been with him and that he had been the catalyst. He found her transformation to be vital and could only help her survive in a cold, cruel world. . . . Joe had even taught her to be streetwise."

I don't have to give him any credit, he's already taken it.

I DECIDED THAT the way out of my problem was the way I'd come in. The newspaper. I put together a packet of the photocopied articles with a cover letter, explaining my personal relationship to Howie and Margo, and put the oversized envelope in the mail to the Stamford *Advocate*. A few days later, I picked up the phone and called John Breunig, the city editor, and left a message. I pitched a story about Margo, linking her with Howie, who may or may not have killed her, and back again to the corruption in the city, which almost certainly killed Howie. The thirtieth anniversary of Margo's death was coming up in July 2006, and I used that as a hook.

"Thirty years is a long time to keep a case open," I said. "Call me if you're interested."

He was. John read the articles and got back to me, adding another angle to the cold case: The paper had not done Margo justice. "We didn't do a very good job, did we?" he said. "The articles treated her only as a victim. We can do better than that." He wanted the *Advocate* to make it up to her and paint the picture of a whole person, even at this late date.

Because I knew Margo and Howie, John assigned the story to someone with no personal ties to the subjects, someone who could bring a fresh perspective, and, of course, someone with real journalism skills. Not only could his reporter Zach Lowe open those doors, he was local, so he knew where the doors were. John asked me to write a companion piece in the form of a personal essay.

Zach called a few days later, and I told him what I knew and how hard it had been to find any information outside the *Advocate* articles, especially from the police.

"Did you file a Freedom of Information Act request?" he asked.

"No," I said. It never even occurred to me.

But, as I have pointed out, it is probable that even if I had filed one, my request to the Stamford police would have been denied. Even Zach, who was well known by the police and exercised his FOIA rights with them often, came up against resistance. They told him they needed to get an okay from the state's cold case department, and that response was not forthcoming. After a few weeks, the police chief, a fairly recent appointee, agreed that wasn't necessary after all and gave the go-ahead. That done, they had trouble finding the file. But after much perseverance on the paper's part, it suddenly appeared. Zach went to the police station up on Bedford Street to collect it, but they said the copier was broken. Since he could not make a copy of the file to take with him, he had to spend hours in the archive room going through the microfilm, writing notes by hand.

I filed my own FOIA request a couple of weeks later and received permission as well, but when I got to the police station, Margo's file was gone. Gone, gone, gone. The archive officer couldn't find it.

"That's so strange," he said. "The case was just out for Zach."

I was there with this officer in the archive room while he was looking for the canisters, and he seemed truly perplexed, not just going through the motions with a smirk on his face. All he could come up with was a single roll of microfilm with the narrative of the finding of the body in the July 14, 1976, police log and the subsequent exhumation. It was a horrible copy, barely legible on the microfiche screen. So, I have never seen Margo's case file. First, it was inaccessible, then it disappeared completely.* Much of the information and personal connections I have assembled to help me write Margo's story I owe to Zach's efforts.

And it continued to be an effort. The investigation began to feel like walking through a graveyard of headstones whose names and dates had long worn away or had simply sunk forever back into the earth. Zach had trouble finding many of the people involved in the case—or they wouldn't talk to him, or they were dead. In the article about Howie's death, the paper mentioned that Lt. Consadine was the acting chief detective that day. Three weeks later, Consadine was officially appointed acting chief after Kinsella resigned in the heat of Anthony Dolan's first police corruption article. Presumably, this meant that Consadine was thought to be a clean cop. He was still alive when Zach began his research and was living in a nursing home. Zach made an appointment to meet with the old chief to find out what he remembered of the case, but then Consadine died the night before.

"Are you sure this is safe?" my husband asked. I shrugged. I doubted there was foul play but hoped that just the mention of Howie and Margo hadn't pushed an old man over the edge.

Zach traced Margo's mother down in Florida. She hung up on him. I called her. She hung up on me. Zach found one of Margo's two younger sisters, but she refused to talk as well. I had hoped that an inquiry from someone taking an interest, wanting to get the story straight, might have been welcome. But no. After Margo's death, her sisters had to grieve, then move forward toward their waiting lives. The brambles had to be allowed to grow

*Recent efforts to gain access to the file have been unsuccessful as well.

over the past if there was to be any future for them. They, after all, knew Margo as whole and vibrant, and that's who they grasped onto.

When Zach called Velma, Howie's mom, she pleaded with him not to write the article. "I wish the paper wouldn't. No one will ever know what we went through," which was a different response from the one I got from her a few years before, when she wished me luck. After the article was published, she wrote an angry letter to the paper asking why they had to bring all this up again. She said she was glad her husband was dead so he wouldn't have to relive the pain.

I have struggled with the pain my curiosity has caused, but if we allow the victimized and murdered women of the past to be forgotten, without even questioning who killed them, we normalize their deaths. And the truth is, "all this" had not been brought up before. Zach's article changed the death of Howie from a man killed in a liquor store holdup to that of murder suspect. The two families knew he was a suspect, but the rest of the world didn't. Until Zach's 2006 article, Howie's and Margo's names had never appeared in print together. Never. What society could not do in life—keep black men and white women apart—it had done in death.

EADING THE police interviews with Margo's friends and tracking a few of them down, Zach confirmed that Margo wanted to work alongside Howie, the street doctor, and be his equal partner in selling drugs. As it is, it's difficult for one half of a couple to deal without the other's being involved on some level, what with the phone calls, deliveries, and late-night visitors. She was never arrested, but she was an active participant in the family business. In the early 70s, Joe and Howie had been able to work out of Norwalk as independents, but by 1975, when Howie was doing business on the streets of Stamford, he must have been dealing directly with the mob. According to Dolan's articles, in that city, in those days, there was no other option. If Margo wanted to be Howie's equal, then it meant close association with the city's underbelly in order to do what the bad boys did, which was sell drugs. Equality was our mission.

ZACH AND I—or John, the editor, and I—would talk or email during the weeks of their research, and I kept expecting some information to arise that would cast a doubt on Howie's being the killer. I was still holding out hope that it was all different than it appeared to be. But such was not the case. While there were a couple of curveballs, Howie was really the only suspect. There was no random killer, but neither was there a racist killer, which was some small relief.

Why Howie was never charged became more of a mystery. I hoped that Zach's article might reveal that the detectives involved with Margo's murder case—McNulty, Lee Odle, and O'Connor—were dirty cops, but they seemed clean enough, although I did find the article from August 14, "Mayor orders City probe of extra payments to cops." A check of salary records back to January showed that the police department's three highest ranking officers, including O'Connor, all received extra pay authorized by the police chief, beyond their contracts. We might never know more about that, since there was no follow-up. And I thought for sure that Angris, the cop who shot Howie, would be found to be connected to the mob, but no.

I removed a few sentences from my companion piece, sentences that claimed I was not completely convinced Howie was the killer, and sent it to John. It wasn't the essay I had started six years before, when I began my mission, but it was what I had when I left my expectations behind.

————————————

THE *ADVOCATE* ARTICLE "Cold Case, Who Put the Arrow in Margo Olson?" with my sidebar essay, "A Friend Remembers," was published as a front-page feature of a section of the Sunday paper, July 23, 2006, thirty years after Margo had been buried, very close to what would have been her fifty-fifth birthday. I would turn fifty later on that year. With the publication of Zach's article, Margo blossomed from black and white into Technicolor, like Dorothy pushing open the gates of Oz. Zach found some of her old friends, people I never knew, and they spoke warmly of her, a creative, daring woman who was far more than a victim.

Moreover, unlike the first time, when the *Advocate* didn't even put Margo's photo in the paper, John had driven over to Darien High School, pulled out her 1969 yearbook,* and copied the photo. I had gone to the Wilton library for her yearbook when I first started the project, because the 1976 article that identified Margo said her mother lived in Wilton. The paper, not sharing anything personal about Margo, never reported that she grew up in Darien and went to Darien High. "It's a small thing," John said, "but after thirty years, it feels right to finally be able to publish an image of her." He said the saying she had chosen to go with her photo was heartbreaking. *Love is something stranger than eternity.* In the photo, Margo's soft face is fully revealed, her tidy hair pulled back by a narrow band, and she smiles shyly at the world. I had never seen that smile before. Below, the page was filled with a collage of all the articles I'd read in the Ferguson basement, tracking Margo's path from Darien high to the potter's field.

There was information that was new to me, and more that fleshed out the bones of what I did know. Some questions remained unanswered, such

*The 1969 yearbook motto: We dare to be.

as where her body was for over a week before it was discovered, but there were answers to questions I didn't even know I had. One of these was the correct time Margo was last seen alive. The article of July 26, 1976, had been wrong. It was 2:30 p.m., not a.m., when Margo left a party on July 3. Like me, the original reporter must have assumed that a murder like that would take place at night. It is why I always envisioned some dark, drugged-up scene, with the actual killing happening at dawn's first light on the Fourth, because no matter the circumstances, an archer needs light to shoot. But Margo had been at one of the many daytime celebrations taking place all over Stamford on the third, when the tall ships were parading toward New York City for the actual holiday. As they sailed down Long Island Sound, the coastal communities held their own celebrations to watch them. Stamford even had its fireworks that night to avoid competing with New York's show on the Fourth. I had always imagined, once I allowed myself to do so, that Margo died soon after those fireworks, but that wasn't the case. She was killed in broad daylight as the ships were sailing past, while everyone in the city was looking out to sea, their backs to the land.

It seems that Margo and Howie fought violently and repeatedly over on Court Street; it was not just a single case of assault as reported in the July 20 article. It was just as Carol told us. The police had been called to the apartment a few times over the winter and through June 1976, sometimes by Margo, other times by neighbors. Maybe even Carol called, or one of her daughters. The walls were so thin in that place, it must have seemed as if they were brawling in their living room. Howie and Margo must have been oblivious to the noise of their own disintegration. According to Margo's file, on June 21, 1976, neighbors reported screaming, and when the police showed up they noted a smashed television, stereo, and window. During this visit or a similar one, an officer noticed a hunting bow hanging on the wall.

I never saw that bow, but I wasn't looking either. Joe and I rarely went to their apartment. We would run into them around town but did not socialize as a foursome. Mostly, I saw Howie alone, when he came over for cards or to just hang out and smoke a joint with Joe. I kept my distance. But if I *had* seen the bow on the wall, would I have thought back to the card game and Howie's professed murder weapon of choice? Perhaps, but I still wouldn't have thought he was serious. Never would I have worried about Margo's safety.

Susan Mingus had written in her book that Charles practiced archery in his NYC studio, shooting arrows from a longbow into a target propped against the wall. I asked her about this hobby. She said it was just part of Charles's protection against a hostile world. Did archery make Howie feel safe? Maybe it made Margo feel safe, even pleased, that her man could protect her, not thinking it was Howie she'd need protection from. Maybe the bow hanging on the wall, sleek and lethal, was a shared object of some warped fantasy.

My Catholic upbringing introduced me to many saints from a young age. Saints as I knew them usually had frightening, transformative lives that often led to perverse deaths, stories that did nothing to inspire us to become a saint ourselves. In many Christian religions, you choose a confirmation name: for Joe's AME confirmation, he chose Angel, and mine is Teresa, after Teresa of Ávila, of whom I knew nothing except that she had violent visions that somehow translated into spiritual bliss. In one of these visions, in 1559, an angel repeatedly drove a hot-tipped arrow through her human heart, God's open wound. Teresa wrote:

> I saw in his hand a long spear of gold, and at the iron's point there seemed to be a little fire. He appeared to me to be thrusting it at times into my heart, and to pierce my very entrails; when he drew it out, he seemed to draw them out also, and to leave me all on fire with a great love of God. The pain was so great, that it made me moan; and yet so surpassing was the sweetness of this excessive pain, that I could not wish to be rid of it.*

Even in catechism class, we knew there was something so weird about this that it couldn't be touched. Later, we would understand that this weirdness was love and sex gone off the rails.

MARGO MISCARRIED two days after that beating on June 21. I didn't know she was pregnant, and if Joe knew, he didn't let on. The article did not say how far along her pregnancy was. Zach's research indicated there might have been other miscarriages.

Here is a fact about domestic violence: If there is violence in a relationship to begin with, it often escalates during pregnancy. In fact, the leading cause

*Teresa of Avila, *The Life of St. Teresa of Jesus*, translated by David Lewis (Westminster, Md.: Newman Press, 1962), 29.17. The vision is the subject of Bernini's sculpture *Ecstasy of Saint Teresa* at Santa Maria della Vittoria in Rome.

of death among pregnant women is not complications from pregnancy, but murder. I didn't know that then. I know it now, from years of working with the many domestic violence programs that had sprung up in the 80s. But back in the 70s, there was very little public awareness, and for me, no personal awareness.

But they did not break up after the beating and the subsequent miscarriage. Margo courted death and stayed with Howie. That too is standard for victims of abuse. It was a relationship that was demeaning, demoralizing, and dangerous, and she stayed. Even if you know something is killing you, yanking it out leaves a terrible hole. His very presence shielded her from the world, which, for some reason, seemed to hold more terror for her than he did.

A week later, at the end of June, their relationship finally ended, and it was Howie who cut Margo loose. This was a surprise. I had not understood from reading the original archives that Margo had moved to Norwalk alone, that she and Howie had broken up. The 1976 articles never said ex-boyfriend.

The details of that breakup were not in the 2006 article, but according to Zach, it was in the file, told from the viewpoint of witnesses as well as from Howie's interrogation by the police. Margo and Howie had a huge blowout at the tennis courts at Cummings Park, a public beach on Shippan Point, the wealthy part of Stamford. Howie had a car full of money, anywhere from five to seven thousand dollars. It was unclear what they were fighting about. It might have been the same old fight we all were having. She wanted to be his equal and was cut out of a deal that she had helped set up. Maybe they didn't need an excuse to fight anymore. At any rate, she jumped into his car and drove off as if blinded, screeching and swerving down the road. She crashed into a tree by accident, or she crashed into a tree on purpose, but the result was the same. The crash stopped the car. She was unhurt, and Howie got both the car and money back safely, but he was insane with anger. It was almost certainly money he owed to his drug distributor, who would eat his liver if he didn't get paid. When Margo drove the car away, he must have had a vision of his own demise.

It was over. They both moved out of Court Street that week, Howie to another apartment in Stamford, and Margo to Norwalk. They had been together for just about a year.

T THE PARTY where Margo was last seen, the hosts and friends reported in the original 1976 articles became Ilene Lush and Kenny Clinton. Ilene was Margo's best friend. Zach found her name in Margo's police files, and then she found me before I could find her. I should have known Ilene, seeing as how we lived in Stamford at the same time and belonged to the same club of interracial couples. Ilene had joined the club at fifteen when she moved in with Kenny, who knew Joe. Ilene knew Joe. But since it wasn't a club where we were ever encouraged to find other members, our paths never crossed.

Today, Ilene is a Goth knockout, artist, writer of one-woman shows, and successful NYC tile and stone dealer. Right after the 2006 article, we met in Port Chester, New York, on the Connecticut border, where she had recently moved from Brooklyn. Oddly, I had been in her building before because my sister's boyfriend lived in the loft above, so she didn't even need to tell me how to find her. Kismet, as we used to say. She was born Ilene Marsha Weinburg, a local Jewish girl whose father, a former marine, owned a deli in Stamford. She left home when she started seeing Kenny and went on to live with him for thirteen years. I love this woman. She knows how to adapt. I also admire her ability to wrap her mind around people who might be just a little bit off. She had a higher tolerance for freakiness than I did, hence her friendship with Margo.

On the evening of July 2, 1976, Margo, wearing a denim jacket, had arrived at Ilene and Kenny's apartment in Stamford for a weekend of bicentennial celebrations. The first thing Margo did was call Velma, Howie's mom, asking her to tell him that she was in town and wanted to see him. Being a dealer, Howie might have had a phone at his new place, but either it wasn't hooked up yet or he told his mom not to give the number to Margo.

Since I hadn't known that Howie and Margo had broken up, I could not have known that Margo sought Howie out. She was after him. In the few days between the time of their breakup and the time of her disappearance, Margo was telling friends that if she couldn't have Howie in this life, they would be together on the other side, quoting Hendrix, "If I don't meet you no more in this world, then I'll meet ya in the next one."

ILENE ONCE WROTE TO ME that many people need to be taught the difference between violence and passion. "A lot of us don't know. And when you can't get the reaction out of someone that you want, like love, you hunt, peck and poke around until you get a passionate reaction, like anger. We all have been guilty of this one."

Margo once showed up at Ilene's door, naked except for a blanket wrapped around her and her hair all matted. "Do you think he'll kill me next time?" she asked.

"People do die in these situations," Ilene said. They do indeed. And yet, when Margo was free of Howie and had escaped with her life, she continued to seek him out. The dynamic of the abused and abuser hadn't been broken yet, but maybe there was something in her that made her determined to make it work, one way or another. Same as me. Same as Ilene. Women of all colors, young and old, often put up with a great deal from their partners, but we had the additional onus of something to prove. We stayed, determined to prove society wrong about interracial relationships. All of us, so damned determined. We were not, NOT, going to let our parents or society tell us what to do.

We'd let our boyfriends do that.

THE NEXT DAY, JULY 3, Margo ate fried chicken and coleslaw at the bicentennial lunch Ilene was hosting. During this party, Howie, who had been telling everyone he never wanted to see Margo again, came to Ilene's door around two. Margo didn't have to call him, and he didn't have to appear. But there he was.

Ilene was wary. She and Kenny would not let Howie in. They did not want a scene. When Margo heard Howie's voice, she met him at the door, where they immediately started fighting. Ilene told them they had to take that shit elsewhere.

A few hours later Margo was dead. Ilene has had to live with that for the rest of her life.

ACCORDING TO THE police files and to people that Zach talked to, Howie's story about what happened after they left the party kept changing. To some friends he lied outright and said he hadn't seen Margo since June 30, when they went their separate ways. But in both of two very long interviews with the police, he acknowledged that he had gone to Ilene and Kenny's apartment and that he and Margo left together. Once outside, she agreed to go for a ride with him. He must have invited her. He said that during the drive, she asked him for money and he gave her a $100 bill. She didn't want it, she wanted much more. She wanted her equal share. He claimed she was all spaced-out and asking questions like "What's happening here? What's going on? Why did we leave Ilene and Kenny's place?" He said that after five minutes, he kicked her out of the car in front of the Lemon Tree restaurant on Summer Street, and that he never saw her again.

As for his whereabouts the rest of the day, Howie told the police that he was at his sister's house for a family BBQ. None of his family, friends, or even an off-duty Stamford police detective who was a guest at that party (Watson Walker, the brother of Howie's sister's husband) remember seeing him there. But people did see him earlier, at his parent's house, before the party. Velma had already told Howie by phone the night before that Margo was looking for him. He arrived the morning of the murder and went to his bedroom, where a bow and quiver was hanging on the wall. It is unknown whether it went missing from the home during the time of the murder, or if it was even the same bow that had been seen by the police at Howie and Margo's Court Street apartment a few weeks before.

There was another family BBQ on the Fourth where people definitely saw him, because he brought attention to himself when he showed up with an ugly cut on his finger. Mostly, Howie insisted that he couldn't really remember what happened in the twenty-four hours after leaving Ilene's apartment. He said he had smoked too much weed and had blacked out. That's a lot of weed, especially back in the days when it was mostly vegetative matter and precious little THC. He'd have to have smoked a bale of it.

LOGISTICALLY, it is hard to understand what may have happened at the potter's field. The police had determined that Margo was tied in an upright position to one of the trees at the arboretum bordering the field. She would have had to have been. If she were unrestrained, she would have fallen to the ground with the impact of the first arrow. She was facing her assailant, since the arrow entrances were through the chest, not the back. Except for a shoulder injury, there were no signs of a struggle either at the site or on what was left of her body. Subdued by drugs? Love? Another person? By the knowledge that she'd have Howie to herself soon enough if he actually went ahead and killed her?

IN THE WEEK AND A HALF before the discovery of the body hit the paper, Howie was casually asking friends (other than Ilene and Kenny, who he'd been avoiding) whether they'd seen Margo. One of these friends was Joe. According to police notes, Howie went to our apartment on July 7, four days after Margo was last seen at Ilene's, but before her body was discovered. I was probably at work, but maybe not. Just because I can't remember Howie's coming by doesn't mean I wasn't there. I wouldn't have any reason to make a special note of his being there, since no one knew Margo was dead, and only Ilene suspected she was in trouble.

When Margo failed to return to the party after she walked out with Howie, Ilene was sick with worry. "I thought Howie had her at home chained to the toilet." She called Olson's new landlady in Norwalk, but she hadn't seen her either. No one knew where she was. No one reported her missing.

THE SINGLE ROLL OF microfilm from Margo's file that the officer was able to find in 2006 after I filed the FOIA request was the report of finding her body on July 14, 1976. At the top of the police log page is written "Possible homicide or other act of violence." There was not much in it that was different from what the police told the newspaper. The name of the officer who wrote the report is missing, cut off at the top. The White family was walking from north to south down the dirt path of the potter's field. There was a strong odor coming from the west side, in a clump of pine and cedar. They saw a hand and foot protruding from a freshly dug grave. It was 11:10 a.m.

The first reporting officer was Mackey, and a couple of minutes later, Lieutenant Hogan arrived at the scene. Larry Hogan was the head of narcotics at the Stamford Police Department, in more ways than one. The two of them tied off the crime scene with rope, then they called the medical examiner and ID Bureau. More officers arrived, including Captain O'Connor, who was put in charge of the case.

At one o'clock, officers finally arrived with four shovels, gas masks, and rubber gloves, with Gallagher Funeral Home right behind them. At two, the *Advocate* photographer arrived. According to John Breunig, the editor at the *Advocate*, the photographer had a reputation for arriving at crime scenes before the police did and taking photos that would violate today's journalism standards. But this time he was told to stay at the command post area set up on the dirt road. John said a picture like the one of Howie's dying in the mud would not be allowed today, so I am glad to know the police were protecting Margo. Or someone.

One of the officers noted that there were no weeds growing on the disturbed earth, an indication of how very fresh the grave was, and then they began to dig. Soon, the body was partially uncovered and measured at 5'8". Margo's right hand was over her face with the palm pointing up. She wore a blue-and-white blouse—later referred to as a green halter top—and blue jeans with two little zippers down either side.

In the July 17 article, Captain O'Connor said that police were assuming that the woman and her killer were locals, saying that "whoever it was had to know Stamford well enough to know about that potter's field." That seems logical for the killer, but since when does a victim get to choose her place of execution? I think they decided she was a local because of her jeans. As Margo's body was being exhumed, one of the police officers, a Lieutenant Toscan, said the jeans, with the two little zippers, were exactly like a pair he had purchased at the Buffalo Shop on Atlantic Street in downtown Stamford. This was in the days of unisex jeans, when they were pretty much all made for men, even ones with seductive little zippers down the side.

The police log said that her dirt-packed hair appeared to be golden blond and that she was wearing a black leather wristband and wristwatch. On her ring finger she wore an interlocking ring. I wondered whether Margo had felt married to Howie. I wondered whether he put it on that finger. The missing Chinese slipper was found thirty feet from her exposed foot.

At 2:22, the rain, which had been threatening all day, began, and Margo was covered with blankets. There had been heavy downpours between the time Margo died on July third and the time she was found on the fourteenth.

Rain washes away evidence. The police didn't want any more of it slipping away.

While they all waited for the shower to pass, they found "a razor-type blade" stuck into a cedar tree south of the gravesite. An Exacto knife, like a box cutter? It might have had nothing to do with the murder. The rain stopped just as Dr. Gross, the medical examiner, arrived to photograph the body and an officer brushed dirt off Margo's face by hand for him. At 4:03, the state police arrived, along with Dr. Henry Lee of the University of New Haven, a technical advisor to the state police. He is now famous in forensic circles. In 1995, he was the expert put on the stand for the prosecution in the O. J. Simpson trial.

Everyone stared at Margo, and then they shrugged.

Once they were gone, Margo's body was moved to the hearse by the undertakers and driven away to Gallaghers Funeral Home. At 5:31, all the officers at the scene left and resumed duty, wandering off to arrest some guy for nonsupport.

WHERE WAS MARGO'S BODY before the Whites found her? The police were quite certain she'd been killed at the potter's field, but when she was found, Dr. Gross said she'd only been in the grave a couple of days. That is ten days unaccounted for, unburied. Recorded in the police log was a conversation with a couple of young boys who rode up on bikes to see what was going on. These brothers, sixteen and twelve, were regulars along the path, and they told the police that two black males and a white female were in that area having a party some time near the end of June, on a Saturday or Sunday. The men wore pimp cloths and were in their 30s. The female had pale, golden blonde hair and wore pants and a waist-length coat. It was sometime around noon. The vehicle was compact and yellow. Howie and Margo had a yellow bug, like us, but the boys said it was a Toyota. The boys were not sure how many of them left in it.

Howie didn't wear pimp clothes—meaning, a suit with long jacket and a wide-brimmed hat popularized in the 1971 blaxploitation film *Shaft*, as in the shaft of an arrow or the shaft of a penis or getting shafted. It was about the black private detective who saved Harlem from the mob, and I never saw anyone in Stamford dressed like characters in the movie, certainly not Howie, who was still wearing leather-fringed vests from the 60s. Having said that, the boys might have believed that any clothes a black man wore were pimp clothes by virtue of skin color. There is also the possibility it was Margo doing a drug deal on her own, without Howie. But if the boys got the date right, no matter who that trio was, she was not murdered at the end of June. It was, however, around the time that she and Howie were splitting up, and she would have hardly been in the mood to party with him, as the boys called it. Smoking pot? Sex? Who knows. The point is, this was a spot where people often came, day or night, for illegal or intimate business, and it was a spot where young boys rode by to spy on the generation ahead of them, just as Denise and I had once done. If a rotting body had been lying around for ten days, it would have been found long before the Whites came upon her.

According to the police interviews, Howie traded cars with his sister between Margo's disappearance and her discovery. He would not have given her a car with a body in it, and besides, at that point, the car would have reeked of rotting flesh. In the same way that the *Advocate* had a drawing of a thermometer on the front page to show how cold it was in January, in July they had a thermometer to show how hot. Where can you hide a body in hundred-degree heat?

All of which begs the question, if the killer—or killers—had the opportunity to dispose of the body far from the crime scene, why didn't they? And when they finally returned with the body, for whatever reason, why not do a decent job of burying it? Taking into consideration that murderers are always in a bit of a hurry, Margo's grave still left a lot to be desired, covered as she was in less than a foot of sandy soil. She barely even fit lengthwise into the shallow space someone made for her. The gravedigger didn't go nearly deep enough. It's almost as if the burial had been half-assed on purpose.

ON JULY 15, 1976, the day after the Whites found Margo in the potter's field, Ilene saw the *Advocate* headline, "Mystery shrouds finding of body," she read out loud in horror. "It's Margo. I know it's Margo."

"It's not," said Kenny, according to Ilene. "It can't be."

"Oh yes it is." Ilene still had the denim jacket Margo wore when she arrived on July 2. A few years later, Ilene left Kenny, and when she left him she left everything. This included the few remaining physical mementos of Margo, a series of photographs Ilene took of her in a graveyard holding up her hand, showing off the pentagram on her palm, the same palm that was facing up in her grave. In Ilene's rush, she also left Margo's jacket behind.

I have some pictures of me from when I went to visit Christie in Colorado in April 1977. I was still with Joe, but he had gone to London without me to buy his first speculative car, so I took the opportunity to look at mountains. Most of the pictures are of the Rockies, but a few are of me, taken by a mutual friend. In one, I was sitting on a rock wearing a hat I crocheted myself. I was also wearing jeans, work boots, and a denim jacket that was already worn out when my mother bought it for me at the Salvation Army back in high school. I still have that jacket. The denim is almost sheer, and it is shredded at the wrists. I always thought my own girls would want it, but no. It was never in style at the right time. Maybe a grandchild will want it someday. I can't give it up.

As Ilene says, "A girl doesn't leave her denim jacket behind unless she thinks she's coming right back."

———————————

DR. GROSS PERFORMED the autopsy on Margo's body the next day, and that was when the arrowhead was discovered. But in her file, unearthed during police interviews with her friends, Zach discovered another wound, a deeper, psychic one, that could never be found with a scalpel. Margo had told Ilene, as well as a number of people over the years, that she'd been sexually abused by a family member. She used the word "rape." She did not say whether it was a single incident or ongoing over the years. Zach did not put this information in his 2006 article.

I have to wonder whether the police told the family about this discovery. Did they ask them what they knew about it? Probably not. Most likely, they doubted its veracity. Back then, women were rarely believed when it came to childhood sexual abuse and incest. Or I should say, believed even less than they are today. It was unspeakable and unspoken.

I kept the essay I wrote for the 2006 article in the *Advocate* up on my website so that anyone looking for Margo could contact me. Sometimes they do. People who have never forgotten her sometimes stop to wonder, like me, whether her case was ever solved. A childhood friend and neighbor of Margo's wrote that she always believed that incest was going on in Margo's house. Margo had told her as much, and this was well before she started using drugs. This friend witnessed the fear. If Margo told an adult at the time it was happening, no one seems to have listened, and when she told friends later, no one knew what to make of it. As I have said, by the time I met her, Margo could seem strange, so when she revealed her secret, friends might have thought it was an odd flash from a tripping brain. And if they believed her, what could they do? In the 70s there were few support systems and organizations available to help incest survivors, as we learned to call them in the 80s. Before that, we didn't call them anything. They were invisible. As adults they often suffer from self-loathing and an exaggerated willingness to remain in dysfunctional or abusive relationships, often with a need to escape the body with substance abuse.

Go away, go away, go away.

ZACH SAID THAT Margo's police file indicated that as soon as the July 17 article "Hunting arrow was used to kill unidentified woman" appeared, the phone line at the police station got very busy. Everyone in town who ever had any association with a bow and arrow was ratted on. "Police are investigating this arrowhead to determine where it may have been purchased." They went to every store that sold hunting supplies in the area and came up empty-handed.

And yet, in the file, Zach found a letter that claimed a man had purchased a three-pronged arrowhead from Caldor's with a stolen credit card in April 1976. And it wasn't Howie. The man in question was David McKeithen Jr., the son of a former black police officer, David McKeithen, who had left the force on corruption charges in the 50s. Zach had reported this information as being in the 70s, but the paper made a correction after the family took umbrage. David Sr. had a brother, Angris, the officer who fatally shot Howie in the liquor store holdup. According to a letter written to the police from a woman named Robin Lord, who claimed to be David Jr.'s ex-girlfriend, David Jr., Angris's nephew, had purchased the arrowhead. I have not been able to track down Robin Lord or find any evidence that she lived in Stamford under that name.

If the police had followed up on that letter, they did not report the results. Presumably, they had already gone to Caldor's, which had a hunting department. There was no follow-up to this statement in any of the articles, and there was nothing in the file about any interviews with store clerks, Caldor's or otherwise. Neither was there anything to indicate whether the investigators ever talked to David Jr. If they did, what they learned never made it into the file. Maybe they never follow up on vindictive letters written by ex-girlfriends. Who knows?

David moved to California shortly after Margo's murder. Zach tried to reach him for comment when he was writing the article and never heard back. Ten seconds after the article was published, he called. He talked to Zach, saying, yes, he lived with Robin Lord for a few months, but they weren't boyfriend and girlfriend, as was written in the paper, and he didn't even know Margo Olson. He didn't say whether he knew Howie, and, he added, he was going to sue the paper for defamation of character. As far as I know, he didn't.

Lt. Ligi, the only officer involved with the investigation who was still alive in 2006 (and the one who appears in Joe's novel chasing Jackie Robinson Jr. to his death), told Zach he didn't remember the McKeithen tip but said it would be "strange" for police not to pursue it. Ligi was a clean narcotics cop and was consulted in Margo's murder case only in matters to do with the drug dealing. He could only say that maybe the follow-up never made it from paper to microfilm. And then he shrugged.

*A*CCORDING TO THE original 1976 articles, three days after the mystery body was first discovered, an anonymous male called Margo's mother and the police department, and the body was a mystery no longer.

Who was this man? It would have to be someone who knew how to get in contact with Margo's mother. I had hoped Zach might find a clue to his identity in Margo's file, but no. There's a small chance that the caller could have been Howie. He might have been sociopathic enough to want to play games. But considering how frightened he looked when Joe and I found him in our apartment, I have to assume he would have preferred that the body remained unidentified. Besides, according to the police file, Howie was nervously asking his friends the leading question of how long they thought it would take for police to identify the body. Joe would certainly have been one of those friends, if not the first, that Howie would turn to for answers. During the course of this research, I have sometimes wondered whether Joe was the anonymous male caller. But I don't think so. He wouldn't have known Margo's mother's last name, and he would never be anonymous. He would want the credit.

———————

THE POLICE SUMMONED Ilene to the station to identify Margo's effects and to talk. Ilene, in turn, called Judy Hall, Margo's best friend from college, who drove up from New Jersey. They went together to the station, shaking. Howie was nearby, watching who went in to talk and for how long. Ilene saw him drive slowly by, glaring at her as she and Judy went through the door. Zach, who had heard it from one of the old guys at the *Advocate*, had told me that the first time Howie was brought into the old police station on

Broad Street to be questioned, it was an eight-hour interrogation. He was so shook up that afterward he got into his sister's green Dodge (he had traded cars with her the week before) and made such a spectacularly wide U-turn that he crushed a wooden birthday cake in the traffic island, a red, white, and blue display erected by the Chamber of Commerce to celebrate two hundred years of American liberty. Later, Howie hid behind this damaged cake as he cruised Ilene and Judy. It might well be why Joe arranged to have my police interview elsewhere.

Ilene told me she had "unbelievable clarity" at the police station. On the desk was a file with "Howard Carter" written on the side, three inches thick, dating back to 1967, predating by a year when he met Joe, and just two years after he graduated from high school. On top of the file sat the matching bandanas that were still in the shape of Margo's wrist and neck. These were not, as one might think, restraints used in her murder, but fashion accessories meant to display our solidarity with the masses. We wore bandanas around our necks, our wrists, and hanging off our jeans, tied to a belt loop, like laborers.

Also on the desk was Margo's blue-faced watch with roman numerals, which was mentioned in one of the original articles. It was lined up on O'Connor's desk with all her other jewelry. Ilene remembered the watch well, a Timex with cornflowers on the face, because she'd recently noticed that Margo had lost weight and the watch was hanging loose on her wrist.

FOR THE NEXT FEW DAYS after the identification of the body, Howie was all over the place. He was falling apart. He said he was leaving the state and yet stayed put. It was as if he were waiting for something to happen. At the same time, the police records indicate that he was telling friends, "I never leave a trail," without actually saying he did it. Just in general, you know, he never leaves a trail. He was simultaneously bragging and denying. You can't have it both ways, Howie.

Not long after Margo's funeral, Howie's friends, organized by Joe, did a murder intervention, asking Howie point-blank if he killed her. I had no idea this had happened until Zach told me it was in the file. Afterward, Joe called the police to tell them that Howie denied doing it. For all I knew, the intervention was done at our apartment while I was at work. Apparently, according to Zach, Joe contacted the police quite a few times in the weeks after the murder, helping with the case, ingratiating himself with them, and distancing himself from Howie. Joe did not want to get pulled into Howie's maelstrom. His name was inside that three-inch-thick folder. They had lived together, dealt drugs together, and got busted together. Since the drug business was now run by the mob, of which Joe was certainly aware, he couldn't create enough distance. This would explain Joe's fear surrounding Margo's death, why he skipped right over it in his book, even decades later.

AMAZINGLY, even though Howie was extensively questioned by the police and his story was full of holes, they seemed not to have enough evidence to charge him with murder. DNA testing was nonexistent. It was not enough that Howie was a known archer or that a hunting bow was seen on his wall by an officer on a domestic violence call or that one was found hanging on a wall in his parent's house after the murder. There is no way to tell the last time a bow was fired or whether the arrow had been shot by a thirty-five-pound bow, one capable of hunting big game, such as the one Howie's mother handed over to the police with who knows what heart-shattering pain. That bow is probably still sitting on some evidence shelf in the bowels of the old police station, where some officer left it, scratching his head. Death by arrow is so archaic, so rare in modern times, that it was never resolved whether the weapon was a longbow or a crossbow, or even if she was stabbed, à la Teresa of Ávila, instead of shot. There is a whole science of ballistics to tell us exactly what gun was used in a crime and when, but a bow and arrow? No one seemed to have a clue.

Still, Howie, a known toxophilite, had to do some pretty fancy dancing to explain away the arrow found in his recently ex-girlfriend. He suggested to the police during one of his interrogations that Margo had killed herself by digging her own grave, laying down in it, then stabbing herself twice in the heart with an arrow before covering herself up with dirt. In this way, he claimed, the blame would fall on him, whom she wanted to destroy.

Although this scenario begs the question of what happened to the broken off shaft that should have been in her hand or how you go about burying yourself after you're dead, it was true that, (1) someone might have wanted Howie destroyed, and (2) Margo was suicidal. Howie and Margo moved out of Court Street at the end of June and went their separate ways, Margo to Norwalk, the next town over, and Howie to Atlantic Street, a few blocks away in Stamford. He also seems to have had an apartment on Chestnut Street, for which he collected several rent deposits through an *Advocate* classified ad to raise quick money. How he didn't get killed by one of the people he'd scammed, I don't know, except he must have been planning to leave town fairly soon. At any rate, according to a police interview with Howie's and Margo's old landlord, when Margo returned to Stamford for the bicentennial weekend, she went to the Court Street apartment before going to Ilene's. When the landlord went to inspect what he thought was going to be an empty rental, he found her there with her head in the oven and the gas on.

And yet, Margo's old friend from Fairleigh Dickinson, Judy Hall, had told police that Margo had called her that same day "in good spirits." Margo gave Judy her new address in Norwalk and said she was going to see Howie and ask for blood money for all she'd had to put up with in the time they'd been together. Money can't buy love, but Margo must have thought it could buy some justice. Or else she just wanted contact. The dream of love was still a tug on her heart. She was grieving for what might have been. *Le coeur a ses raisons que la raison ne connaît point.*

Howie had another theory about Margo's death. Zach wrote that during the interrogation, Howie claimed that there was a contract out on Margo's life from when she lived in New Jersey. What Zach did not include in his article was that Margo was bisexual. Judy Hall told the police that Margo had slept with a woman in town named Amy, and that Amy's husband beat his wife up when he found out and threatened to kill Margo, but Judy didn't think he was connected to the mob and had never heard of a contract. According to police notes, two of Howie's friends claimed that Margo had mentioned a contract, but those were Howie's friends.

Joe might have been one of them. In the single appearance of Margo in his novel, he had made a point of mentioning that she had ties with "a family" in New Jersey. He implied it was a cult, like the Manson family, but there is no evidence to suggest that cult members came to Stamford to kill Margo. For what? Why? Maybe he was also inferring that it was a Mafia family contract, as Howie told the police. But it must have been a long-term one, because the Amy incident was over five years before Margo's murder.

But maybe there was a contract on Margo, much closer to home, and much more recent.

WHILE THE POLICE were interviewing Howie and talking to friends, Margo's family mourned. There was a big, beautiful funeral at Noroton Presbyterian in Darien, in a church full of irises, Margo's favorite. It is a purple flower named after Iris, the Greek goddess of the rainbow, traditionally planted on the graves of beloved women, in hopes that the goddess would transport their souls to the Elysian Fields, the place of perfect happiness. Someone sang John Denver's melancholy "Sunshine on My Shoulders," Margo's favorite song. I was not there. I wasn't even told there was a funeral, but Ilene said that Margo's friends sat in the balcony and cried and cried. The Stamford detectives on Margo's case attended the funeral to listen to the chatter. They came up to Ilene afterward and said, "We didn't know." Ilene asked him, "Who did you think we were?"

The police, like most of the world, probably assumed Margo was just another drug dealer's girlfriend, living on the edge, sleeping with black men. Expendable. They must have been surprised to find out that she was held so dear. Ilene told me, "We were their children, we were everyone's children at the time."

The Olsons buried their daughter and tried to forget. Margo was dead, and even though I didn't go to her funeral, I buried her too.

After the police finished tearing apart Margo's apartment in Norwalk, where she had lived for all of two days, Ilene went there to pack up her things. She wanted to spare Margo's mother ("she was lovely") the onerous task. The mom let her take what she wanted. I'm guessing the sisters kept one or two items as a memento, if they kept anything at all, and then sent the rest to the Salvation Army. Ilene took a blue coat with a striped lining. She never wore it. It fell on the closet floor, the cat had kittens on it, and then, when she moved out of Kenny's house years later, she left it behind with everything else.

Afterward, Ilene was determined to lead a normal existence. Morbid, but normal. Her hobby these days is corresponding with women on death row. She has an ashtray in her loft that is circled with little human skulls.

I'm not making any judgment, not me, the woman who spent her Paris vacation wandering through cemeteries.

I HAD FINALLY WRITTEN an essay and gotten Margo's story out in the world, but I felt I had somehow failed in my mission. Something did not jibe. My story had gone from black and white to color, but it was still woefully out of focus. It had also grown to the size of a book. But a book about what? After years of research, I had a much more fully formed Margo, but the story wasn't that different from what I had before: A black drug dealer almost

FIGURE 4. Christie and JoeAnn in Colorado, 1977. JoeAnn is fake-eating something they find very funny and wears the denim jacket she still owns. Courtesy of Cindy Kitchen.

FIGURE 5. (*Left*) Publicity photo of Joe's mother, singer Georgia Louis, circa 1984.

FIGURE 6. (*Right*) Margo Olson, Darien High School senior portrait, 1969. Copyright Darien High School.

certainly killed his white girlfriend, then got killed himself by a police officer during an armed robbery. What could I possibly hope to accomplish by writing that story? Nothing. I had to shape meaning out of what seemed to be meaningless violence. To justify the pain I was causing the families by resurrecting the dead, I needed a payoff. Something that would make some sense of it all.

Sense. What was that? My mission was stalled. During this time, I had a dream where I was holding a plastic baggie of dark remains, all that was left of Margo. In the dream I was thinking that she couldn't be "found" because of time, and what was left was unrecognizable.

PART 3

And Judas cast down the pieces of silver in the temple, and departed, and went and hanged himself. And the chief priests took the silver pieces and said, It is not lawful to put them into the treasury, because it is the price of blood. And they took counsel, and bought with them the potter's field, to bury strangers in.

—The Gospel according to Matthew 27:5–7

*I*N 2014, I picked Stamford up by the scruff of its neck again, determined to be done with it. Either I could make sense out of the story or I couldn't, but I had to see it to the end, and in this effort to reframe my mission rose a question I had never asked, Why would Howie kill Margo? It was a question I had never really considered, just as for so many years I had not asked, "Who killed Margo?" In the beginning, I had been so sure that Howie didn't kill Margo, because I knew him, and I refused to believe that anyone I knew could commit a heinous murder. But after all I'd found out, I had to concede that Margo had been killed by Howie and it was no accident. As for motive, my feeling was that a man who beat his girlfriend on a number of occasions didn't need an excuse to kill her. It was obviously all about control and possession. I saw her murder as the sick act of a violent creep, whom she'd made the fatal mistake of loving. What else was there to know? A breakup is the most dangerous time for a woman in an abusive situation, but the thing is, Margo had already escaped, even though the breakup had been his call. She had moved to another city. Not only that, but he wasn't tracking her down, she was tracking him. Was that a reason to kill her?

Ilene told me she thought Howie did it for the thrills, that he was pushing all the edges. She likened what he did to *Rope*, the Hitchcock movie, where two college boys kill a friend for the excitement, justifying it with a deranged interpretation of Nietzsche. They stuff the body in a trunk in their apartment, then have their friends over for a party, including their philosophy professor, Jimmy Stewart. They shake out a white linen tablecloth, straighten out the edges, and serve them dinner on the trunk. Ilene thinks Howie wanted to serve dinner. He wanted to know what it felt like to have a dead body, a dead body of a white woman, in his possession. He wanted the power. It would go a long way toward explaining where her body was for over a week.

But I don't think so. Howie was not wrapped in privilege as those two rich college boys were, thinking they could get away with murder. A dead body is a hot potato. And in the heat of the summer, it is highly perishable and putrid. No. Life had ceased to be fun and games for Howie long before.

WHEN I TRIED TO imagine the chronological steps of what might have happened when Margo left Ilene's with Howie, the more convoluted it seemed. How did the scene in the car morph from Margo's saying "I want money" to Howie's saying at the potter's field, "Stand still while I tie you to this tree out in the middle of nowhere so I can step back a few paces and shoot you with an arrow." Without her full cooperation, it would be almost impossible to pull off alone. A bow-and-arrow killing is not just a macabre and ritualized ending: it is complicated. There are many more steps than just lifting a gun and pulling the trigger. The murderer would have had to chase her, catch her, subdue her sufficiently to be able to tie her to a tree, and then get some distance from her to shoot, an act that in itself has many deliberate steps. Even with an accomplice, it would not have been easy to do.

I opened up the file cabinet and revisited all my materials. In 2006, John Breunig had given me a thick 175th anniversary issue of the *Advocate*, which had a prominent section about Tony Dolan's Pulitzer Prize–winning series. The article in the special issue stated: "The reports were explosive. Honest officers and other sources provided information showing a Stamford detective was an agent of the Carlo Gambino crime family in New York. One of his men, a sergeant, was the biggest drug pusher in Stamford, arresting other dealers to eliminate his competition from the streets. Five other Stamford police officers were tied to the Gambino family." Many of these officers were running their own rackets, including burglaries. Remember the aluminum siding? They were ripping off liquor stores, camera stores, and construction sites all over the city, and no one was being prosecuted.

I was already familiar with the corruption overview, but I had only read the first few in Dolan's series, starting with the one on October 22, 1976, when Police Chief Kinsella resigned. I knew there were more articles, written over a two-year stretch, and I always meant to read them all but never did. I believed that the first articles told me everything I needed to know, that Howie was killed by the police because he would have taken half the mob-infiltrated force down with him if he was charged with Margo's murder.

Then, with my new question about *why* Howie would kill Margo in mind, I read the rest of the articles. A librarian at the Ferguson had sent me photocopies of the Dolan articles, which at this point they had in a separate file called "70's Crime, Stamford," and by the time I finished reading them, I had readjusted my focus. This adjustment was enhanced during one of my regular forays on the internet, where I found a new book on the subject, *Rogue Town*. It had just come out in 2014 and was written by Vito Colucci, one of the "honest officers" cited in the anniversary article, a Dolan informant. Between the book and the articles, the mob transformed from a faceless group into individuals with motives and histories of their own.

For so long, I had seen Howie and Margo as opposing forces. In the big picture of their story, I had been looking at racism, misogyny, domestic violence, mob influence, civic corruption, urban renewal, and corporate flight from New York City, all of which played a part, but I was putting the emphasis in the wrong places. Once I began to frame Howie and Margo as couple up against outside forces, not just one another, I was ready to venture a working narrative on why these two young people were dead.

———————————

AS I HAVE SAID, I was only vaguely aware of organized crime in Stamford while I lived there. Joe and his friends often talked about the mob and how they controlled everything in the city, but I couldn't tell how they knew, and I often thought they were being paranoid. I had only one oblique brush with the mob that I knew of, and I had to take Joe's word for it that that's what it was.

I was sitting in our VW in a bank parking lot waiting for Joe. I was in the driver's seat, but the car was not running. I was perfectly aligned in my parking space minding my own business, when a large, boney Cadillac maneuvered out of its slot from across the lane and slammed right into my car. A white woman in her forties with corn-colored hair, dark roots, and brown-penciled eyebrows got out to look at the dent she had just made in my left rear fender. I don't know how she maneuvered herself out of the car, her pants were so tight. She ripped into me about how the dent was my fault because I was in her way. By the time Joe came out, the two of us were nose-to-nose yelling at one another.

"Joe," I said when I saw him. "The bitch hit the car. Go back in and call the police."

Joe did not look at me. He was staring at the woman, and he looked at her car—her undamaged car—and smiled at her. He addressed her by a name I do not remember except he addressed her as Mrs. He apologized, and I almost dropped to the ground.

"I'll take care of this," he said, meaning me. He took me by the shoulders and started turning me away from her. "You have a nice day now." Again, he called her by her name.

She didn't seem to know who he was but showed no surprise that he knew her. I was now struggling to get out of Joe's grasp, but she didn't even look at me. With a smile, she turned as sweet as honey, thanking Joe as she slid back in her car in her camel-toe pants. I was sputtering, and Joe was holding onto my arm so I wouldn't run after the Cadillac as it left the parking lot.

"What? *What?*" I asked.

He shook his head and walked over to our damaged car. He touched the dent with his hand, laughed, and got in the passenger seat.

I got in the driver's side and slammed the door. "What was that all about?"

"Her husband's a mob boss. You'd only get the police angry if you called them. They'd end up locking you up, not her."

"They would not. She hit my car!"

He lit a Newport, and the car filled with smoke. "Are you more concerned with a dent in your car or a dent in your head? Let's split."

I grumbled and started the ignition, steaming from the injustice. I would never have thought Joe would cede ground to anyone, least of all someone who had just smashed into our only means of transportation. Yet I never wondered how Joe knew who she was, this wife of a mob boss. "What a bunch of bullshit," I said. When I backed up, the back tire rubbed against the dent.

Joe looked out the window, watching the woman drive away down the road. "I've done her a solid. That might come in handy someday."

ET'S IMAGINE for a moment a scenario informed by all I have learned so far. Let's say Howie and Margo meet at some party in Stamford the summer of 1975, not long before Joe and I will meet in September. Like Joe, Howie has been known to date just white women. We could say that Margo is his fuck-you to white hegemony, but I think it is also fair to say that Howie, like Joe, believed that white women were willing to cut more slack for black men than black women were, and that would make Howie's life more copacetic.

And Margo, with her bisexuality and appetite for adventure, seemed willing to date anyone but white males. If it is true about the incest, maybe she even wanted to stick it to the family member she claimed raped her and the rest of the family who could not protect her. Sometimes, you search for mates to work out earlier, toxic relationships and hope they don't kill you in the process.

At any rate, Margo soon becomes Howie's own pretty pink thing, as Howie had once called me, and they move in together, first in one or the other's apartment, then, in early 1976, to Court Street. I believe this is the first time either of them had made such a commitment.

Howie has an interesting hobby. Archery. Target practice, either alone or with like-minded friends, usually takes place at the Bartlett Arboretum, adjacent to the potter's field, where there is room and privacy. Margo is intrigued, she likes the medieval aura of a bow and arrow. She learns how to use one and takes up the sport herself, going with Howie to smoke weed and practice. She wants to be his equal in all things. Who doesn't love Diana, Greek goddess of the hunt? A Saint-Gaudens bronze statue of her used to sit on top of the old Madison Square Garden in New York. A cast now rests uptown in the Metropolitan Museum, where I have seen her. Beautiful and resilient, she sets one foot on a sphere and leans into her shot, allowing for the coming recoil.

Margo makes candles and jewelry and picks up a waitress shift here and there, not using her recent degree in childhood education. Maybe she feels she was not cut out to be an elementary school teacher after all. Or the job market is just that bad, there are no teaching jobs to be had. Howie was dealing drugs, mostly pot, some acid, a bit of hash. Thai stick. Gummy dabs of opium. What have you. For years he was running his own operation, as he had done with Joe. But things have changed. Private entrepreneurs are no longer tolerated. He now works for the head of the Stamford Police Narcotics Squad, Sergeant Larry Hogan, an agent of the Carlo Gambino crime family. Hogan ran the gambling and prostitution industries in Stamford, as well as the drug trade, along with his regular duties as head of the department's vice squad. He had a crew of at least five Gambino operatives on the force, but most of the force knew something was going on. They differed in how much they knew and how much they actively or passively participated in the bribes and hush money, but they all knew something fishy was afoot. It was impossible not to. Hogan and his men were so brazen, giving gambling dens a heads-up when clean cops were coming. Organized crime would have taken a piece of the pie as small as the one in the garage where Joe and I used to go.

Hogan would dispense personal information on the clean cops to dealers so they could blackmail them or threaten their families if they found themselves in a tight place. Howie would be one of these dealers. All in all, the rank and file on the force stayed quiet either with money or fear or disbelief. Police Chief Kinsella, the former postal worker, went along. I am unsure what was in it for him, but it must have been plenty.

It got so bad that a few cops, like Vito Colucci, who wrote *Rogue Town*, were quietly breaking the thin blue line and calling the aggressive young reporter at the *Advocate*, Tony Dolan. They called anonymously, independent of one another and against their internal code of honor, to give Dolan specific details of the corruption. They felt he was their only hope, and they are to be commended.

Hogan and his men controlled all the drugs going in and out of Fairfield County with unwavering diligence. They stabbed or shot their rivals. Any dealer on the street who did not buy directly from them and on their terms was simply arrested. They were key witnesses for the state in many drug trials so as to put their competition in prison. In this way, they tied the hands of the district attorney, who was loath to launch a grand jury investigation against such valuable assets. All of these arrests arranged by Hogan made it look like the DA was coming down hard on the drug trade. It made him look good, and he was a man with political aspirations.

Under this threat of violence or incarceration, Howie had come into the fold. Like Joe, he had never wanted a straight job in the white world. Unlike him, Howie ended up working for the Man in the worst possible way.

Soon after they became a couple, Margo, through Howie, began to move some pot for the benefit of the mob too. The danger and challenge of working in close proximity to organized crime might have tickled her enormous capacity for risk. At first, she might even have gone with Howie to do pickups on the eighth floor of St. John's Towers, where Hogan was running his hands-on drug operation. And it wasn't just pot. Heroin was shipped there from New York to be cut, bagged, and distributed. Having this spacey, upscale white woman on the scene, so out of her element, was something that could not have made Hogan happy. Howie began to drop Margo off at Ronny and Leila's, a couple of floors below, then go upstairs to do his business. This couldn't have made Margo happy.

ONE OF THE surprising things I learned in *Rogue Town* was that Hogan's right-hand man, Duke Morris, was a black cop. I had read about Morris (Officer X) in Dolan's corruption series in the *Advocate*, but I would never have suspected his color. Hogan and Duke worked together in keeping all of Stamford's illegal enterprises in Gambino hands. During this time, Vito Colucci was knowingly arresting gamblers and dealers who had Hogan's protection. They weren't going to stop him! No sir. Then one day, while Vito was pulling out of his driveway, he paused to check for traffic, and when he looked back, he found Duke Morris standing by his side with a gun pointed at his head. It was only because Morris realized at the last moment that Colucci—in the days before car seats—had his young daughter on his lap that his life was spared. Soon after that, late in 1972, Morris resigned from the force, possibly for some outrageous crime that even Hogan could not cover up, since it was probably harder to make excuses for black cops.

Colucci happened to be on duty at the train station on the day Morris was leaving town, and Morris approached him. Vito put his hand on his gun, but it turned out Morris just wanted to talk. He confirmed that Vito had almost lost his life that day in the car, if not for the little girl. But that was then. Before his train arrived, Morris wanted to explain himself. He told Colucci that there were very few "colored officers" when he started, and the ranking officers used his race and knowledge of the black neighborhoods to send him where the other cops couldn't penetrate. Stamford was his town. He had been forced to arrest his friends and family. He felt as if he'd been poorly used, and that's what turned him into a dirty cop. The train arrived, Morris said goodbye, and off he went to New York City.

In an article on December 10, 1976, four years after Morris left Stamford and a few weeks after Dolan's corruption series began, Morris was arrested at Gimbels, in Stamford, for stealing coats. He was identified as the "Officer X" in the Dolan article and as living in New York City. Aside from the coats, he must have been in town to check in with Hogan, for whom he was probably still working, just not as a police officer anymore. The article said he retired in 1972 for medical reasons after complaining he suffered from hallucinations and repeatedly had contemplated suicide, despite electroshock treatments and tranquilizers. He was granted a pension of $7,000 a year.

He did not do any jail time for the coat theft. The last anyone knew, he had spent some time in prison in New York, and after that he was eventually shot and killed by other drug dealers. Maybe he was even killed by one of the uncooperative dealers he had testified against in his Stamford days, someone who had finally gotten back out on the streets with a mission of his own.

MORRIS MIGHT HAVE BEEN Howie's entry into the mob, recruited after his bust with Joe in 1971, which would go a long way toward explaining why Howie did not do any time. Unlike Joe, he was not at Columbia and did not have Manny Margolis as his attorney. Even though Howie was busted in Norwalk, the district attorney would have been the same as for Stamford. Morris might have pulled some strings. It was a favor that Howie would have to repay, but having to buy from Morris and Morris only would not have felt too much like coercion. It must have felt fairly safe, one brother helping out another in a tough business. Morris probably cut Howie some slack or gave him special attention, but when Morris abruptly left town late in 1972, Howie had to deal directly with Hogan. No more cozy arrangements. Howie holds his nose and keeps his head down, buying from Hogan, turning his product over on the street, doing what he must to stay out of trouble.

Time goes by like this for Howie, dealing and partying, partying and dealing, and then Margo comes into the picture in the summer of 1975.

Because of her affluent Darien connections, she and Howie were probably able to expand their client base and product line, which makes Howie happy even as they remained closely tethered to Hogan. They are being shaped by criminal forces around them, bound together with no way out. But they don't know that yet. I imagine that they think they still have control over their lives. Margo likes being in on the danger, together, with her man.

It is Howie who sees the light first. Maybe because Hogan distrusts Margo, he tightens the reins, and Howie soon realizes he can't even take a piss without permission from Hogan. He is repeatedly put in his place and made to jump, doing pickups, delivering, selling, all on command. Quotas. For a man who has always run his own show, he was small potatoes now. He was nothing. He takes out his frustrations on Margo. The beatings begin, if they have not already, and they escalate in the spring of 1976, when Margo tells him that she is pregnant and is keeping the baby. She wants to start fresh, she wants to give this child a perfect, normal childhood, the one she learned all about when she was in college. Let's assume this meant she wants out of the drug business. Let's assume she wants Howie to get out too. But it is far more complicated than she thought. Howie can't just walk away, and she should have known that. She can't just walk away either, but neither of them knows that yet. But they know something is not right.

In an email from Margo's childhood friend, she wrote about seeing Margo and Howie in the spring of 1976:

Margo was so vibrant and funny and loving when I knew her those ten plus years. So strange to see her near the end the way she was. She once came to the drive-up window when I worked at Merchants Bank in Norwalk. It was a separate building and she asked to use the bathroom; she needed to wash and actually removed her shirt and washed it in the sink. She appeared at my apartment with Howie one night complete with dinner preparations just out of the blue. I had never met Howie, and there was something that made me feel very afraid. I think they needed somewhere to "crash." I felt as though something very dark and dangerous had entered the apartment with them. Understand that it had nothing to do with his being African American, my regular friend-base resembled the UN; on the contrary, it was something around him, his air of secrecy, of sizing you up when he looked at you or spoke to you and, I don't know, just an overall feeling of, maybe, "dread"? Given the size of my apartment, it would have been impossible to accommodate them both. I remember thinking when they left that I hoped Margo would be safe, in my gut I didn't believe that she would be, but I had no idea what would happen months later.

After one of Margo's beatings, she goes down to the police department and files a complaint. No formal charges were ever made, but that could have been Margo's decision. Victims of domestic violence are often afraid of what their abusers will do to them if they press charges. Margo might have also been afraid of what the police would do to her. Since Howie was a Hogan dealer, he had some protection against arrests of any kind. She was just a girlfriend and had no protection against anyone.

In spite of this, she had not been afraid to call the police in the heat of violence. But on June 21, she did not call the police in time. A female friend, possibly the wife of the landlord, drove her to the hospital, and she lost the baby two days later. When Margo was released, she would not go to her mother's house, and she did not have the resources to go elsewhere. She returned to Court Street. With mixed feelings on both sides, she and Howie made up. Maybe Howie even felt some remorse. According to Ilene, Howie kept a little book with him at all times in which he wrote notes to himself and kept a list of baby names, one of which was Dank. Who keeps a list of baby names who is not expecting to use it someday, as strange and grim as the names might be? He must have wanted a baby, and yet his violent actions resulted in his not having one. Freud would say Howie killed Margo because he felt guilty about the miscarriage. "In many criminals, especially youthful ones, it is possible to detect a very powerful sense of guilt which existed before the crime, and is therefore not its result but its motive."

Oh, Sigmund. I love how your mind works, but no. Maybe if it were a death by fist or gun or some other instant gratification weapon, I might consider this option. Hate, love, insanity, many things can explain an act of passion, but it is hard to pin a bow-and-arrow killing on any of those mental states. It is so premeditated. So cold. It is as if it were a death staged for the benefit of others.

———————

HOWIE AND MARGO'S reconciliation didn't last long. A few days later, they are at Cummings Park, right down the street from where Hogan's boss, the drug kingpin of all of southern Connecticut, lived. His territory extended from Portchester to New Haven. This is where they have their final fight, and whatever it is Margo wants from Howie, she wants it bad enough to threaten to go to the FBI or the newspaper or both with what she knows about Hogan's operation. And she knows a lot because she had been a part of it. She might even be willing to turn state's evidence, and what a lovely witness she would make. It would all come out.

You know what? Never mind the FBI. It's Howie she wants to screw, not Hogan. Maybe Howie hadn't been all that forthcoming about sales data with his boss, and she knows it. If she were to tell Hogan, Howie would be one dead dealer. In the heat of their fight, she screams this at Howie. Margo, wrapped in white privilege and affluence, must have felt protected from the fallout of her words. She runs for the car and drives away with the money before ending half way up a tree.

They break up for real this time. Hogan, who has always been nervous about Margo in the picture, hears about the incident in the park and that Howie almost lost the money because of that flake. He is all over Howie. All over him, up and down. Howie assures him that it's cool. The bitch left town and won't be back. She won't cause us any trouble.

Hogan is not so sure of that. In spite of her loopiness, he has picked up on her defiant intelligence. The Darien bitch was just the type to threaten to go to the Feds with everything she knows if she didn't get her way, and at this point, she knows far too much.

After the 2006 article, the *Advocate* got a few responses, but only one email had anything that could be called new information, and John forwarded it to me. It was not for the letters page, but, as the anonymous writer put it, for John's edification only. This man dated Margo's sister Suzie in high school. He became friends with Margo later on but lost track of her after she graduated from Fairleigh Dickinson. He talked to Suzie just days after Margo's funeral, and he wrote that "the family knew much more about who was responsible for Margo's death than has ever been reported."

The story he got from Suzie was that Margo had a boyfriend who was connected to organized crime. That would be Howie. "She said there were complications, and that Margo had been trying for some time to extricate herself." True. She might well have left Howie a few times, but she kept going back. "She had a lot of knowledge of this guy's activities and associations and she had threatened to use this information against him. Suzie had little doubt that her big sister had been killed for knowing too much, or for failing to understand the gravity of making threats like this to this individual."

Yes, yes, I thought when I first read the email. I knew all about the mob.

But I too easily dismissed the suggestion that Margo's was a mob execution. The bow and arrow was a weapon peculiar to Howie, after all, not the Gambinos. At that point I had not yet understood that working for organized crime made even a low-rung player like Howie an inseparable part of an ingrained culture. I had not reasoned that Hogan might capitalize on Howie's hobby to his advantage—and to Howie's great disadvantage.

The email went on. "If organized crime was indeed involved, it is understandable that the family would be reluctant to say anything to authorities for fear of their lives. Your cold case story saddened me. It also enlightened me to the fact the cold cases may sometimes have something to do with police suppressing their complicity in the crimes."

———————

AMEN TO THAT. "Don't dig too deep" might have been the motto of the Stamford Police Department. Howie was the ex-boyfriend, with a history of domestic violence, the police saw a bow and arrow on his wall, he had no alibi and no sane excuse, and yet he wasn't arrested. For all the work they seem to have done on the case, they never charged Howie with so much as a parking ticket. Maybe they knew him better than anyone and were sitting back, just paying out enough rope to let him hang himself. No matter which way I looked at it, the facts reinforced my opinion that the police wanted Howie dead instead of arrested. And when I changed my focus, I could easily speculate that the police were responsible not just for Howie's death but for Margo's as well.

———————

WHEN ILENE contemplates Margo's death, she always "sees" a third figure. Not that she has a suspect, only that she was standing near Howie at a party once, and he saw a man coming toward him who owed him money for pot. He turned to Ilene and said, "I'm going to kill him," which she brushed off as bravado. But after Margo was killed, she wondered whether Howie would need or want an accomplice to a murder, someone to witness him in the same way he pulled Ilene into his drama at the party. It's a stretch, but murder is such a stretch to begin with.

But I'm not so sure Howie was in any position to be pulling anyone into his drama. I think by the time he and Margo walked out of Ilene's apartment, it was he who was being pulled into a larger, more dangerous drama by forces now well out of his control.

*L*ET'S SUPPOSE Hogan tells Howie that if Margo comes back to town, she must be eliminated—by Howie. She is his problem. A very big problem. Hogan strongly suspects that Margo might want to retaliate against Howie by reporting the dealing operation outside his protected circle of police and district attorney. A girl like that, who can be sure that she wouldn't tell the FBI. So, if he finds out that she is back, and he has to hear about it from someone else, then it's Howie who will be taken care of. Capeesh?

Howie swears. It's cool, man. It's cool.

Margo moves to Norwalk on June 30 but returns to Stamford two days later to spend the bicentennial weekend with Ilene and Kenny. But first she stops at the old Court Street apartment and puts her head in the oven. Was she serious about suicide? Maybe, when she went back to collect a few forgotten things, she felt hopeless. She was still reeling from her recent beating and subsequent miscarriage. Her hormones were plunging like a postpartum stone. Who knew how she felt about being a mother, and then so violently not? Or maybe she and Howie had always stored their drugs in the back panel of the oven, and she was looking to see whether anything was still there. When the landlord arrives, he either stops her in the act of killing herself, or she lets him believe that to cover up what she was looking for. He claimed the gas was on. It may not have been. She could have just turned it on for effect. Or she may have been truly intent on death.

She leaves without explanation and arrives at Ilene's soon after, on the evening of the second. As she had confided to her old college friend Judy, she tells Ilene she wants money for what she went through with Howie. That night, from Ilene's, Margo calls Velma, Howie's mom, up in North Stamford and tells her she is looking for him. She can be reached at Ilene's.

Velma tracks Howie down to give him that message and to confirm the family's weekend festivities. She asks him to bring a case of soda to his sister's house the next day. After talking to his mother, Howie hangs up the phone and begins shaking with anger and fear, mixed, perhaps, with a sick bit of excitement. He has to call Hogan. Margo is back. What now?

Hogan tells Howie, in no uncertain terms, what has to be done before the stupid cunt gets them all nailed. In Hogan's mind, this will be a lesson to all the dealers' girlfriends and a lesson to the dealers themselves. Choose wisely, keep your trap shut, and the bitches out of your business. He knows Margo had contacted the police about assaults. Hogan sees her as a snitch. He sees her as someone who goes to the authorities when she is agitated. Someone with faith in the legal system. Who believes in justice.

He doesn't need to say all that to Howie, but he does tell him that if he doesn't kill Margo, then he might as well kiss his black ass goodbye. Howie is pushed into a corner of his own making. It is him or Margo. Hogan tells him that he will send help to insure the job gets done properly—their old friend Duke. Hogan knows that this is Howie's first hit. It is a test. If Howie is able to do this, he's capable of much more, making him useful to Hogan in the future. He tells Howie he has to do the dirty work himself. It's his girlfriend. His pretty pink thing.

Howie says he doesn't have a gun.

Hogan reminds him that he's always said that if he were going to kill someone, it would be with a bow and arrow. Here's your chance.

Howie had hoped there might be some other way out of this, but he comes to believe that on the other side of Margo's death lies the end of his troubles. Maybe he even aspires to rise up in the Gambino organization. A made man. Power, money, respect. Who knows what Hogan has promised? Who knows whether, after the initial horror, Howie isn't getting off on the high? This is for real.

Howie wakes up late on July 3 and makes a run to his parents' house for a few things. Let's say he gets the hunting bow off his childhood wall, along with the quiver of arrows, a rope, a tarp, and a couple of beers. He does not want to be seen, but Velma corners him, as moms are wont to do. She reminds him about the soda. And don't be late. He drives downtown to Ilene and Kenny's apartment. Ilene does not want to let him in. Unaware that Margo had called Velma the night before, she asks Margo whether she wants to talk to him, and she does. Margo is relieved that Howie has responded to her call. It is a good sign. Maybe she hopes they can get back together.

Maybe Howie still hopes he can just convince Margo to leave Stamford forever. Go away. Go away. They pick up their fight at the door, and Ilene sends them both away.

Howie and Margo fight in the car, of course, but that's nothing new. She wants money, she wants the respect and equality it signifies. She wants it enough to make trouble if she doesn't get it. Let's assume Margo reiterates her threats. She'll go to the FBI, she'll go to Hogan about Howie's skimming drug money, she'll do anything.

Driving north through town in Howie's car, they go by back roads to the potter's field. The lover's lane. Howie has stopped being angry. He is very quiet. Maybe Margo thinks they are going there to fuck and make up. She brightens at this thought. She has her man back. She loves him.

Right here, right now, Howie could save her. He could push her out of the car and say run, do not come back to Connecticut or you will be dead. He could lie to Hogan and, like the woodcutter in the fairy tale, tell him he has killed her and disposed of the body. But Hogan would have found the living, breathing Margo in no time. So, no, it could not have happened otherwise. Howie might have been terrified, but he did not chicken out. As the man says in *Double Indemnity*, "There comes a time in any murder when the only thing that can see you through is audacity." Howie knows that it is him or Margo.

Someone is already at the potter's field waiting. Whoever it is, Duke Morris, some other minion of Hogan's, or even Hogan himself, his job is to make sure Howie gets it done. The last thing they need is to have Margo survive a murder attempt and start talking. For the sake of argument, let's say it's Duke. He has left his car at the arboretum parking lot nearby and made sure no cops are patrolling the area. He needn't have worried. Hogan has already looked at the day's orders and adjusted them as necessary. Besides, the cops have their hands full with parties and events all over the city that day, especially along the shore, where the tall ships were going by, miles away.

Howie approaches the potter's field by way of Scofieldtown Road and turns onto Old Scofieldtown Road, whose barricades had been long removed. He parks. Howie tells Margo he wants to relax, smoke a couple of joints, do some target practice. Cool, she thinks. This is where they usually do archery. This is familiar, normal. A date. We're back together.

She helps him take his equipment out of the back seat of the car, including a paper target. Tack that up on a tree trunk he says, and he looks around. He is sort of sick to his stomach. He can't do this by himself. But then he sees some movement through the trees, and they head that way. Margo doesn't see Duke at first. Howie carries the bow on his shoulder and quiver on his back. Inside the quiver, among the small-pointed practice arrows, one of his shafts has a hunting arrowhead attached to it. Maybe he had traded some pot for it, months before, with his buddy David, who liked to mess around with arrows too. Like Mingus, Howie wanted it as part of his arsenal to protect himself against the dangers of the white world. He wants it in case he ever had to protect himself from Larry Hogan. In a way, that's just what he's doing now. He wishes he were elsewhere. He thinks of his family at his sister's house getting ready for the BBQ to celebrate the bicentennial.

He and Margo walk down the dirt road, turn to the right, and Howie points to a tree. That one, he says. He puts down his bow and quiver. Margo walks over to the tree with the target in her hand. The target is not a bull's-eye. Howie likes to use the kind with a human outline, even though that human always seems to have an Afro, like a halo. Howie walks right behind her. She turns to ask him for the razor blade that he keeps in his quiver for pinning the target to the trunk of a tree. When they pause, Duke steps out from behind the tree.

Margo, initially frozen in confusion, would have turned to run, but Duke grabs her arm and stops her. Howie grabs her other arm and the target falls to the ground. There must have been some struggle. She hurts her shoulder. A professional at restraining criminals, Duke handcuffs her. Margo is terrified. She knows who Duke is. It is serious that he is there. She should not have come back to Stamford. And yet, firmly wrapped in white privilege, she still believes she is only going to be roughly threatened. Warned.

They drag her to the tree and tie her to it. It's truth or dare now, and Margo wants to see how far Howie will go. She does not believe that they—that Howie—will actually go so far as to kill her. She and Howie have played games like this before. He will stop at the very last second, and they will make up. She is not sure what Duke's role is going to be in all this. Maybe he and Howie are going to play good cop, bad cop.

She is fearless, as she has always been. She does not scream for help. Besides, she knows how futile screaming would be in that town, what with Duke in on the game. Duke is happy not to have to gag her. He wants her to be able to talk. He has learned a lot of valuable information in situations like this over the years. Hogan would love to hear what she has to say under duress.

Maybe Margo pleads to be released. Maybe she is just angry and starts saying what she'll do when this is over. Or maybe she has long since stopped caring what will happen to her. She had tested oblivion in the gas oven at their old place. She does not know whether she would have gone through with it if the landlord had not come in. She is not even sure what she was thinking. Going back. Saying goodbye to the apartment. Saying goodbye to life. This is where her story might twist into a gothic fiction, as in Daphne du Maurier's *Rebecca*, where the wife taunts the husband to kill her because she's been diagnosed with inoperable cancer and wants to die quickly. And because she is a spiteful bitch, she wants to take her husband down with her so that he's executed for her murder.

Margo is no spiteful bitch, but she just might want to take Howie with her when she goes, to have him with her for eternity. Howie in the meantime is swept up in the energy of the hunt. He takes out his new arrow and positions it against the bow but immediately cuts his finger on the lethally sharp three-sided arrowhead. He is nervous and is not used to playing with the real thing, only practice arrows. As Howie pulls himself together, Duke secures the rope that ties Margo to the tree after she has loosened herself somewhat by twisting hard with her shoulder. She still has good strength in that side of her body from her tennis days. When she finds herself unable to move at all, barely able to breathe, she hisses to Duke that he has the wrong person, that it's Howie he wants. He's been screwing Hogan by skimming cash off the top of every delivery. She can prove it if he will just release her. Duke tells her to work it out with Howie, then goes off to make sure the area is clear of witnesses.

He tells Howie to hurry the fuck up as he passes him.

———————————

HOWIE WALKS AWAY from Margo, but not too far. A thirty-five-pound bow can do big game hunting, but only at close range. He turns toward his target and nocks the arrow, aligning the groove at the feathered end of the shaft with the string to hold it steady. The red cock feathers are up and the green hen feathers down, so the arrow will fly right. He turns his left shoulder to Margo and raises his bow, the arrow secured on the rest, his left palm a little sweaty on the throat of the handgrip. When his arm is straight and parallel to the ground, he looks down the shaft at his target. He looks at Margo and judges the distance between them. She stares back at him. She loves that she is the very center of his attention at that moment. She is all he sees. She ignores Duke, who is far afield now, keeping an ear out for trouble. Keeping his hands clean.

Howie draws back on the bowstring with three fingers, and in that movement, he transforms his rage against the world into a powerful symbolic gesture. He does it out of fear for his own life, he does it out of pure misogynist fantasy. He does it because he is one sick fuck. He aims, and in the Zen spirit of the art, steadies himself to become one with his target.

Go ahead, she says. I'll meet you on the other side.

When his shooting hand lightly brushes his chin and the bowstring cannot be made any tighter, he lets go, and all the stored energy held in the space between the bow and the string is finally released. The shaft bends before straightening in the fury of flight. It could have happened that at the moment the arrow was undone from its restraint, it was Howie, not Margo, who saw his life pass before his eyes and saw himself transformed from a low-life street dealer into a god who has the power over life and death. He let the feeling wash over him. It could be that Margo in that same instant is more alive than she has ever been. It could be she feels a moment of grace and is ecstatic. All the mind-expanding drugs she has taken in her lifetime could not have prepared her for this, the world coming at her in a peaceful rush, the energy moving toward her as it leaves Howie. The energy has left him. He has transferred it all to Margo, and now she has the power in the relationship, and she will not give it up easily. He can kill her, but in the end she will bring him back to her. In time, he will follow his arrow to her heart.

There is no explosion of sound as with a gun, but it is not silent either. They all hear the whistle of an object taking flight, the sharp intake of air by the archer, the victim, and even the witness, as if no one can quite believe that it is really happening. There is the almost quiet squish and crunch of metal entering flesh and bone, and a mortal gasp. There is the sound of the bowstring reverberating back to normal, all energy spent.

If Margo was calling Howie's bluff, she has lost her bet.

———————————

DUKE WATCHES at a distance. He has participated in his share of murders but has never seen one done by bow and arrow, so he's a little distrustful. He has a gun ready, just in case. When the arrow finds its target, he is somewhat impressed by Howie's skill but soon realizes it isn't enough. Margo is moaning. She's not dead yet. She will be, but they can't wait for a slow bleed out.

He comes over from his lookout and yanks the arrow out of Margo's twitching body with a gloved hand. Her eyes are wide, her mouth open, and she's looking either right through him or right at him. Either way, she's not gone.

Might he stab her with it? He considers this, but no.

He walks over to Howie and hands it to him. Again.

It is not so thrilling the second time, but Howie's aim is better. He can do this. He pulls back and releases. The arrow tears through Margo's flesh and bone again, landing right next to the previous shot. It severs the aorta, and the blood pours out into the world instead of returning to her heart.

Margo dies on July 3, the same day Jim Morrison had died five years earlier. She would have loved that, had she known.

———————————

DUKE MOVES QUICKLY, even as Howie stands stunned, with his mind following Margo out into the universe. Duke shakes him out of his stupor and tells him to help cut her down. Howie takes the blade out of his quiver and slices the rope. She falls to the ground, and Duke tells Howie to pull out the arrow. He sticks the blade in a near-by cedar for safekeeping while he yanks on the shaft with both hands.

It is not that easy. The large arrowhead, meant for deer or elk, is lodged behind the ribs. A hunter would know how to extricate it while cleaning and bleeding the carcass, but Howie is not at all prepared for this part. He did not think it was going to be so hands-on, so bloody. With his own heart in his throat, he puts his foot on Margo's lifeless torso and pulls on the arrow, his hands wet from sweat and blood from when he cut himself, so that the stiffly fletched end rips across his palms as he loses his grip. He begins to wiggle the arrow back and forth trying to move it, but it breaks beneath the surface of the skin and he cannot get to it. He tentatively probes his finger in the opening, but there is no getting it back. His weapon is now part of Margo's heart. His own blood is now part of her. He holds the broken shaft of the arrow in his hand and begins to feel his transformation not from man to god but from human to murderer.

———————————

AT THIS POINT I could conceivably make a case that Howie is innocent of actually killing Margo. It might have been that the murder itself was committed entirely by Duke. After leaving Ilene's apartment on July 3, maybe Howie dropped Margo in the street after five minutes, as he claimed. Maybe

Hogan or Duke picked her up on the street, as planned. Of course, Howie would have known what was going to happen to her. He would have known she was going to die, but he couldn't have known that Hogan or Duke was going to kill her with an arrow so that her murder pointed to Howie. It's possible. Certainly as possible as my William Tell scenario once was.

But I am no longer on that mission. Howie would have had a real alibi that day if he had not been so busy out on Old Scofieldtown Road. While Howie might have been pressured into the murder by forces outside himself, he is the one who drew back the bowstring, twice. Hogan doesn't want to get his hands any dirtier than he has to. Neither does Duke. Maybe Duke even snapped the shaft off on purpose, leaving the arrowhead in Margo's body so that there is no question whether she was killed by bow and arrow. Howie's sport. Hogan can protect him from being arrested for Margo's murder, or he can make sure he is. He can control which way the investigation points, making Howie his slave for life. Of course, if he finds out that what Margo told Duke about the skimming was true, and he will find out one way or another, then it won't be a very long life at all.

—————————————

NOW IS THE TIME for Duke to take over the logistics of disposing of a dead body. He removes the handcuffs from Margo, while Howie picks up the fallen target and the broken arrow and stuffs them in his quiver. They both forget about the blade in the nearby tree. They lift Margo up and put her in the trunk of Howie's car, where, as instructed, he has spread out a tarp. They lower her onto it. Duke gives Howie an address in Queens. Howie is to deliver the body there, and it will be taken care of. Duke will meet him. Howie feels good about that; he's in the hands of professionals. He wants Margo out of Stamford, far from him.

Howie drives to New York. His heart, still in his throat, is racing, but it is almost over. He meets Duke in Queens, and they drag the body into a storage unit in an abandoned warehouse, where Duke assures Howie that it's going to be taken care of when it gets dark. This costs money, and Howie hands over everything he's got. He does not look at Duke when he says goodbye.

Duke does not dispose of the body that night. He has to talk to Hogan first.

As Howie is driving back to Connecticut, he opens a beer and lights up a joint. He can't get too messed up though, he has more work to do. He has to bring the car and his equipment somewhere to wash it thoroughly, with bleach. He realizes, with a start, that he still has the broken arrow on the floor of the car, dark with blood. In a secluded area off I-95, he makes a small fire using the paper target and twigs and burns it. At first the smoke is sweet with the smell of cedar from the shaft, then acrid with burnt feathers. He pours the rest of his warm beer on the ashes. Much later, that night, while fireworks are lighting the sky over Stamford, he locks himself in his new apartment and gets as high as he has ever been in his life.

In the meantime, Duke and Hogan talk. Duke tells him what Margo had told him about the skimming. Don't put the bitch too far away, says Hogan, and with that, Margo's body becomes a weapon. It can be used to send a message to Howie and the other dealers. Hogan has a few people to talk to first, figures to reconcile. He wants to see how Howie behaves. He wants to see if he is cool, in more ways than one.

You got it, says Duke.

HOWIE NEVER SHOWED UP at his sister's house on the third, but on the Fourth he did make it to his parents' house, where his mother asks, what happened? He tells her that he had stopped in at his sister's, dropped off the case of soda, found the scene a drag, and left. She says there was no soda at the party, and he says well then someone took it. She asks, where did you get that cut on your finger? and he says, opening a beer.

For the next few days, Howie starts getting high all the time with what private stash he has left. He has no money, he wants to work, but Hogan says no. Keep a low profile for a while. Howie gets angry. Killing Margo wasn't his idea. He knows not to threaten Hogan in the same way Margo threatened him, but he is irritable. This is not what he had planned. For quick cash, he borrows money from his mother and puts a deposit on another apartment so he can scam multiple deposits on it. But that won't be nearly enough to start a new life, far away, if he has to leave town in a hurry. The thought of which makes him pause. Except for the brief time with the Jesus freaks in San Francisco during the Summer of Love, he knows nothing but Stamford. It is his world. His town. He thinks of Velma, his mother.

In the meantime, Hogan has sent out feelers, done a few calculations, and sees that Margo was right. Howie has been ripping him off. Just little bits, in that low-life way that street dealers have, but between that and Hogan's hand in Margo's murder, it's cleaner to get Howie out of the way. Hogan is beginning to see signs of public scrutiny and doesn't need a complication in his life right now, a complication like Howie, who might say any stupid shit when he's tripping. Who might want to brag when he's high. Hogan is feeling the heat radiate from the *Advocate*. The newspaper is getting bolder, in spite of threats to Tony Dolan, the new reporter. A kid. Some of the officers are looking secretive. Where Hogan had always been so bold and brazen, he needs to cover his white ass just a little bit more. Where once Hogan thought Howie might be his new black associate—always a useful thing in the business—Howie has not passed that test. He has not been cool. Howie has to go.

Time to bring the body back to the scene of the crime. Howie's crime. And not a moment too soon. After a week in the warm, isolated warehouse, the smell of human rot is beginning to reach the streets. Duke, with who knows what revulsion, brings Margo's body back to Stamford, and in the light of the full moon that Sunday night, he buries her in a shallow grave at the potter's field. He covers her body with a mere twelve inches of dirt, not even deep enough to properly bury a cat. The way she's left, she'll be found sooner rather than later.

The sooner, the better, thinks Hogan.

ON WEDNESDAY, three days later, the Whites find Margo on their family outing looking for paupers' graves, and Hogan shows up at the potter's field one minute later. He arrives to make sure everything was done just so. No surprises. He helps outline the crime scene with rope. He knows just where he wants everyone to look, and where he doesn't. He sends the annoying *Advocate* photographer away.

Imagine Howie's surprise when he reads in the paper the next day that a body has been found at the potter's field. A dead white woman. Howie starts telling friends that it can't be Margo, and he means it. That's not where he left her. That *can't* be Margo.

The next day, Dr. Gross opened up the body and found the arrowhead. Howie reads the paper and knows now, for sure, it's Margo. She has made her way back to the potter's field like an apparition, or a witch, with an arrow in her heart, insuring that Howie, and only Howie, will be tied to the murder. He starts looking over his shoulder. Something is very wrong. He calls Hogan, he calls Duke, again and again. No answer.

A FEW DAYS GO BY, and Hogan gets impatient that Jane Doe is still not identified. He is disgusted with the ineptitude of his detectives. He has to make the anonymous calls himself, the first to Margo's mother in Darien. He knows her name, her telephone number, and where she lives. He knows about the two younger sisters. He has made it his business to know all about Margo, as he does with all of his dealers and their girlfriends. The other anonymous call is to his own police department.

Thanks to his efforts, on the fourth day after her body is discovered, the police—and the world—finally know who she was. "Murder victim identified; probe goes on." And as soon as Margo is identified, Howie is under the gun, just as Hogan intended. Howie's life becomes a horror show. He is one worried man. He is called in to the police station to talk.

Hogan stops in on Howie's two lengthy interrogations and smiles. Howie doesn't have a lawyer with him when questioned. He hasn't been charged with anything, so he can't have a public defender. Why don't his parents help out? They know what's going on. Their son-in-law is related to a Stamford detective. The police have been to their house. Howie knows by now that the mob is not going to supply any consigliere to help him, but maybe he still believes he has Hogan's protection. But if Hogan doesn't give him a high sign soon and tell him what's going on, tell him why Margo has returned to the potter's field, he's going to crack. If he gets charged with the murder, he won't hesitate to pull the fat honky bastard down with him.

Everyone, from the mayor on down to the secretaries at the real estate offices, knows that Howie did it. They worry what it would do to the city's reputation if the news comes out. The mayor and the developers want Stamford to be seen as a safe haven for New York corporations. They do not need a dead upscale white woman on their hands, one who was slaughtered by a black man in North Stamford, right where they wanted CEOs to buy their new homes, CEOs with daughters of their own just like Margo. That would be one ugly fly in the bright civic ointment. So there is no encouragement from city hall to get this black suspect arrested and behind bars. It was easier to turn a blind eye and let Stamford's underbelly take care of its own.

As the summer weeks slip by, Hogan lets Howie feel the heat. A constant threat of arrest follows Howie like a storm cloud. The other dealers feel it too. If it can happen to Howie, it can happen to them. The body has served its purpose, but enough is enough. Howie has bragged to friends that the police don't want him on the witness stand, afraid of what he knows. Time for Howie to disappear. Hogan calls in a favor from someone in his sleazy orbit, Albert Steele, to help in setting Howie up, and tells him the plan. He'll make it worth his while, and Steele knows Howie well enough. If not, he'll get to know him. It's a small town.

Maybe Joe is calling in his own favor. Worried about his friend, he calls Hogan at home, in Redding. Georgia's town. He casually mentions seeing Hogan's wife, Nancy, at the bank that summer. Together they have a chuckle about women drivers and the silly dent in the VW. It's nothing, Joe says. Nothing at all. He mentions that Hogan is neighbors with his mother, who lives with Cal, the Cadillac dealer. Of course, Hogan knows him. It is probably how Joe knew who Hogan's wife was to begin with, through Cal's pointing her out one day. Everyone knows who runs Stamford. Everyone, especially a Cadillac dealer, knows where the power is.

Joe is both innocent and arrogant in this conversation. He does not know Hogan's part in Margo's murder, but he believes Howie didn't do it and wonders aloud if there isn't some way to help him. He mentions that Howie has been a profitable worker for Hogan.

Hogan tells him not to worry. Howie will be taken care of.

As Joe hangs up the phone, he believes he is in on something and puffs up in the reflected power.

STEELE FINDS HOWIE, tells him the word on the street is that the police are about to pounce on Howie and nail him for Margo's murder, whether he did it or not. Howie thanks him for doing him a solid. They commiserate about money, and Steele tells him, as if he has just thought of it, that he knows when the bookkeeper comes to Tower Liquor to count the day's receipts before they go in the safe. An old lady. An easy hit. Just one other guy in the shop, and they'll wait for him to go out back. In and out, and onto the highway. Howie bites. It might be enough money to start again, elsewhere. Steele even has a friend in Atlanta who can put him up for a while. But first they need a gun.

Howie knows a guy who sells them from a room in the Marriott. His blood starts pumping as he steps right into the trap.

Hogan knows his buddy Al Reyes will be working that night at the liquor store, and he knows he is always armed. He gives him a heads up about the holdup, but he can't count on Reyes killing Howie, and he wants him dead. What is needed here is a cop waiting for him as he leaves. Of course, in this plan, it can't be just any cop who kills Howie. No community uproar, please. It has to be a black cop who pulls the trigger, and they are in very short supply. Hogan goes to Angris and shows him a letter from Robin Lord, implicating his nephew in the purchase of the murder weapon, a letter that Hogan might very well have written himself or coerced from Lord. The man seems to have had something on everyone in town, and, after all, according to the file, there was no record of such an arrowhead sale at Caldor's. The point is, Hogan has this incriminating letter. He just shows it, then puts it away. He tells Angris that he has heard that Howie Carter is planning to rob Tower Liquor, and when. If Angris can arrest Howie for the robbery himself, it would be a nice feather in his career cap, and then he can have some control over the evidence in the murder file. No reason his nephew has to be dragged into that messy bow-and-arrow murder. Who wants that? Maybe he has something on Angris as well.

And by the way, Hogan tells the former marine, Howie will have a gun.

HOWIE CANNOT KEEP his mouth shut and tells Joe that he is going to the Marriott on Tuesday night for "business." Joe knows what that means but does not ask him why he needs a gun. He does not want to interfere because this might be part of Hogan's plan to get Howie safely out of town. And at this point, Joe would just as soon have him out of Stamford. It's all too close for comfort. We go to the Marriott for dinner, but really, it's so Joe can see for himself if it was true about the gun. It was. Joe's curiosity gets the best of him. He leaves after one drink at the bar, then goes off to try to find out what the plan was. He finds out soon enough. Howie has gone to the liquor store with Steele, and it all goes terribly wrong. There is no getaway. There never was.

In the middle of the night, Detective McNulty called Ilene to tell her Howie wasn't going to make it and asked her whether he had made a confession so they could close the case. No, Ilene said, he had not. Poor guy can't even die in peace without the Man all over him, wanting something. If McNulty called Joe, I slept right through it. Howie died before dawn, and Margo greeted him on the other side.

AND SO HERE THEY ARE, Howie and Margo, together forever, stuck in an eternal 1976, the Land of Love & Freedom long past, now dark with dirt and blood. It is the story I found, not the one I set out after, a story told in gray, not one so black and white. In a particularly violent decade, maybe everyone is just one very bad decision away from death. And for men, especially black men, that fatal decision usually involves guns; for women, men. But if there is a lesson to be had here, it is not—as society would have had us believe back then—don't sleep with a black man. The lesson is, don't fuck with the mob.

THREE WEEKS LATER, on October 22, Dolan's first article appeared, exactly one week after Carlo Gambino died of a heart attack. One of the shocks in reading the entire Dolan series was finding out that it took years for the city to get clean. Years. The corruption was as entrenched as teeth, and Hogan proved extremely difficult to remove. As I said, he had something on everyone. He was still in the Stamford Police Department in January, months after Howie's shooting, the same month Angris died of complications from his gunshot wounds. Angris had been honored at the Special Police Association's annual Christmas dinner in December. He was quoted as saying that even after the shooting, "he does not believe there are bad kids." When he died, Howie became a postmortem cop killer. They had killed one another. One dead white woman, two dead black men, and Hogan wipes his hands and continues to gather up the money.

Hogan wasn't pried out until the permanent chief came on in May 1977, and even then, he was still a major mob player in Stamford until he died of cancer in the 80s, before he could be brought to trial on any number of charges. With my faith in the power of the word, my belief in the democratic process and justice, I thought all Dolan had to do was write about the corruption and there would be such an outrage, it would disappear. It was why I had not continued reading past the first few articles. I thought the truth had already done its work. I had not understood the mechanics of corruption, how its power is maintained by making sure that community leaders benefit in one way or another, whether they are aware of the source or not. The massive transformation of Stamford's real estate would create incredible wealth for many, so no one looked too closely at who might be suffering in the process or what vile and violent forces were running the street game and skimming off the top. That is the privilege of those in power, to be able to plead innocence. Two weeks after the first article appeared, on November 6, 1976, Mayor Clapes accused the *Advocate* of "yellow journalism." He might have wanted a clean city, but he didn't want to have to acknowledge the dirty one. Certainly not in public. Corporations might reconsider a move to Stamford, and there would be less pie to go around. In April 1978, as the articles and investigations continued, business leaders wrote a letter to the paper asking Dolan to tone down his reporting. They claimed he was making Stamford look bad by creating what they termed a "fantastical illusion," and that he was just trying to create a media event, a crime as "corrupt and morally bankrupt" as those he wrote about.

There were a number of resignations, terminations, and a few convictions, but no one seemed to have actually gone to prison for any of the white-collar crimes, gambling, civic corruption, drugs, or murders. I closed my file. My mission was over.

*J*SEEMED TO HAVE forgotten about the search for me in all this, but it happened all the same. I came along for the ride. The younger me became clearer, and while I was often shocked at my lack of fear back then, I can't say I was making dangerous decisions, just poor ones. The normal ill-formed decisions of youth. For one thing, I put up with Joe's irregular life for too long. Our poverty had been a binding force in the first year, but when Joe got his insurance settlement money in September 1976, the drinking escalated and he was intolerable. Even if he played no hand in Howie's fate, which he certainly believed was going to be an escape, not death, he might have been able to prevent it. He could have talked Howie out of doing something so stupid as robbing that liquor store. It was why Joe's name was on Howie's lips as he lay dying in Joe's novel. "I just have to get in touch with Joe. Everything will be okay." In other words, why the fuck hadn't Joe tried to stop him? But Joe was too busy trusting Hogan. He thought the mob was doing him a favor, when instead, he had handed Hogan the opportunity to get him out of the way. He had been pulled into their vile machinations, and it must have shaken him for the rest of his life. He was the white man's tool. He couldn't drink fast enough, as if he were trying to drown some terrible creature inside of him. For a long time, I had been so busy looking up at the mountain, I could not see I was standing in a drainage ditch by the side of the road.

One day in the spring of 1977, I was in our house in Greens Farms, the area where we lived in Westport, waiting for Joe to get home from a night of partying. It was past noon. I was not consciously packing up my things, although it certainly looked like it. I was going through the shelves and pulling out books, stacking them on the floor, and making a wall of them. One of these was an old textbook from Skidmore, *Gardner's Art through the Ages,* a thick and mighty tome of Western civilization through the scrim of the visual arts, the sort of book that Joe ridiculed as reinforcing white culture. He was right about that. There were few artists of color, and the representations of nonwhites were romanticized and eroticized by the likes of Rousseau. There were many depictions of women, those perennial objects of desire, but few by them.

Sitting on the floor with the book in my lap, trying to distract myself from my anger at Joe, I paged through it, as if searching for something, although I did not know what. As I moved from the Sumerians to the Moderns, I thought of my classes in the darkened auditorium at Skidmore, with the artwork projected on the screen, larger than life. I thought of the life I might have had if I'd stayed, but I was not sorry I left. In the book, I stopped at a painting I remembered viewing, Manet's *A Bar at the Folies-Bergère*. A tightly corseted female bartender looks sadly and directly at the viewer. At Skidmore, I remember it was all about the light, the male instructor lecturing about the way Manet handled the woman in the same manner he handled the champagne bottles and oranges in front of her. In other words, a still life. An object. I placed my hand over her, lifted it, and changed my focus. This time, I paid attention to her, not the light, and saw in her pained face the whole of the human condition, and I felt for the first time in a long time that I was not alone.

And then I felt restless. I had been relying on Joe to hand me what had been inside all along, and it was now scratching to get out. My own life. The search for meaning and purpose might be a universal desire, but it can only be negotiated for oneself, and it was time for me to leave Joe and do just that. He was getting in my way.

I spent so long with the book on my lap my legs went numb. By the time Joe staggered home, reeking of booze, dead on his feet, and had stomped his way upstairs to sleep it off, I didn't even raise my voice. What was there to fight about? He couldn't help the way he was, and I couldn't change him. I could only change my situation. And while I felt defeated, I knew I didn't have to stay with him in the name of racial progress. I closed the book.

It would be months, though, until I finally got out, since figuring where to go was a problem. I was not returning to Pleasantville. I would not let my parents be right, because they were right for all the wrong reasons. I did not want to have to argue my defense, that it had not worked out with Joe because of his color but because he drank too much.

In July 1977, Christie called to say her roommate in Boulder was moving out September 1 and asked whether I was ready to leave. We had kept in close contact over the two years I was with Joe, mostly by letter or the occasional phone call, and I had gone to visit her that April. She knew I was not happy, and while she never urged me to leave him, she held the safety net. So did her mother, who told me I had a place under her roof in Old Greenwich, but that I had to be sure it was the end, because hers was a one-time offer. I never took her up on it because it wasn't far enough away, and I was sure Joe would find out where I was. Old Greenwich didn't have the distance, but Colorado did.

Christie came home for vacation in August, and we went together to tell my mother I was leaving Joe. I was surprised that she got hysterical that I was going all the way to Colorado, because, after all, I might as well have been that far away for the past two years for all she saw me. She screamed, "It's like shooting an ant with an elephant gun!" Meaning, I suppose, that I hardly needed to move so far away from him. Christie scooted on out to the car to hide, and afterward, when my mother calmed down, she asked where Christie had gone. She couldn't understand why she'd left. It was like she had anger blackouts.

At any rate, Joe was hardly an ant. My mother grossly underestimated how hard it was to put down my arms. It was not easy to leave a man with so much potential for life. When I told Joe I was heading west for a while to live with Christie, he took the news without even pretending to put up a counterargument. We were both that tired. Not forever, I said, just a while. I knew I would never return, but it was easier to get out by saying "someday." I was still a coward. But if Joe and I had something to teach one another, I felt I had learned just about enough, and when I walked away, I no longer looked outside myself for me.

Almost two years from the day we met, I left Joe, at the end of August 1977, the week Elvis died. When I left for the Rockies, I carried away with me the pain of wasted possibilities. Joe got me to the airport in time to miss my flight, not to keep me, just to mess with my head. We spent the night at friends' in Brooklyn that night, and I took the first flight out. Next to me was a man (white) who was going to Denver. We dated briefly, and through him I met Gordon, the man I would later marry. White as well. Boulder was a very white city.

When I flew to Colorado with the ring still on my finger, Georgia was the only one crying when I said goodbye. The ring sat in the dark in my jewelry box untouched for many years. When my oldest daughter was at an age to rummage through my things looking to see what she could "borrow," she found it. She recognized an engagement ring when she saw one, so I fessed up.

"Engagements are like pancakes," I told her. "You have to toss the first one out."

Seeing the ring again, though, made me think that Georgia might like it back. This was in the early 90s, and she was still living with Cal in Redding, where I went to see her. I think she was happy to see it. Joe was still alive. Maybe he'd need it again. She smiled as she looked at it in the palm of her hand, then she put it on the table in front of us. We both sighed, and then we shrugged.

———

GEORGIA DIED ON July 3, 2014, the same day Margo died thirty-eight years earlier and Jim Morrison died forty-three years before that. I went to visit Pierre at Georgia's house in Bridgeport, where she'd moved from Redding a few years before, after she and Cal finally called it quits, and he gave me a box of Joe's stuff. In it were some grades from his first year at Columbia (excellent) and catalogs for law schools. Joe had not lied when he told me the first night at the Blue Note that he was looking into applying. The catalogs—dated from 1973, the year after he graduated from Columbia, to 1975, the year we met—were from UConn School of Law and New York Law School. He never applied.

If I met Joe now, I would think, here is a man I am deeply attracted to. Funny, charming, and egomaniacal, with a sheen of addiction and its accompanying mood swings. Only now, instead of running to his arms, I would simply run. That's what age gives you, the ability to run far and fast. Joe's moods were opaque, and part of my attraction to him was the hope I would get a peek behind the façade. That's what love did, presumably, make it possible to see the real person and let your real self be seen. But intimacy did not provide any inner knowledge. Now, instead of trying to reach for that intimacy, I would smile fondly at his charm and his happy ability to let others clean up after him. How nice that must be. I would indulge myself by talking to him for a while at a party, then say goodbye. I would know him. I would know me.

———

ONCE I WAS IN BOULDER, the land of hip progressive culture, the way things were, compared to the way things used to be, was a void that couldn't be crossed. I felt as free as Toad on the road. Growing old is an emotion that can take over at any age, and I'd had it young. I got a job at the Bank of Boulder, where they were attracting new depositors with shiny new rifles, and put Joe out of my mind. But he was not so easy to shake off. He followed me to Colorado seven months after I left him, to win me back. He'd found out I'd broken up with the man from the plane, and he professed to have gotten whatever it was out of his system and was ready to settle down after all. I told him not to come. I was not at all interested in him or in moving back East. Besides, I was already in the relationship with Gordon. Joe said he was coming to talk, and I made plans to be elsewhere. I was working late at the bank when Joe flew in, so a friend went to the airport to pick him up. He told her he was going to marry me, and she said, "huh." When he arrived, he told me he was going to marry me, and I said, "ha." I got him settled in my apartment, where he pulled me down on the bed and tried to kiss me. I brushed it off with another laugh and left to be with Gordon in the mountains. It was the last time I saw Joe.

You will not be surprised to learn that Gordon, whom I married in 1979, was the same age as Joe, another bona fide member of the 60s generation. Even better, he was in the music industry. How cool was that? You will not be surprised to learn that he had many of the same characteristics as my mother, only this time, they were the good ones. The humor, the slight nuttiness, the chatty charm. He was not damaged. We have gotten along.

For years, Joe kicked himself for getting me to the plane late, setting off the chain of events that led to my marriage, as if I didn't marry him because of bad timing. He believed he had *just* missed winning me back.

That's karma, baby.

————————

THE FIRST TIME I TRIED to visit the potter's field, in 2001, I couldn't find it. Old Scofieldtown Road, the former access road from Scofieldtown Road, was gone. More recently, I found it by parking at the Bartlett Arboretum and walking through the woods to where I thought the road might have been, and in just a few hundred feet I found what was left of it. It was early in the spring, so the trees had not leafed out yet. Their bare branches and trunks cast shadows across the crumbled pavement, but I was not afraid. I was ready. The road soon led to a clearing, and there it was. The potter's field. I was expecting it to be unrecognizable. The bracken that the Whites were searching through would have been succeeded by generations of brush, then saplings and trees. But it was open space again. A graveyard committee had cleared the area and exposed the old burial numbered markers dotting the winter-killed grass. More surprising, in the middle of the clearing there was a large stone memorial dedicated to everyone who had been buried in the potter's field, known and unknown. It was erected by the committee on November 1, 1997. All Souls' Day. Margo's grave might be in Darien, but I think her spirit is here, where she died, where she spent three days waiting to be found, and where she saw Howie for the last time.

I tried to imagine where that place was. The tree that Margo had been tied to, where she was shot with an arrow, would have been along the verge with what are now older trees. There is no way to know which one. The cedar thicket where her shallow grave had been found in 1976 is no longer apparent either. It has either been cleared or absorbed into the forest. No matter. I stood with the potter's field at my back and counted out nine paces from the road, as described in the police log. I fixed on a spot where I decided Margo's first grave had been, outside the burial area, not quite fully in the woods. I crouched down and touched the cool earth with my hand.

Come here, Margo. Come closer. Mumble in my ear. Light a candle you have made with your own hands. Let your ring fall apart into thirteen links and form a chain.

I'm sorry I didn't get to know you better when I could.

I'm sorry I didn't reach out through your strangeness. You could have used a friend. And so could I.

The longer I stared at the ground, the more I understood that the greatest potential for danger might be already lodged in our hearts, an open wound, waiting for something to come along and staunch it. Maybe Margo's broken heart was always searching for just the right arrow to fill the empty space inside. Maybe the only lesson that Margo's death can teach us is how to recognize those spaces in ourselves as we go out into the world.

On the boulder was a bronze plaque with a quotation, popularly called "The Impartial Friend," from Mark Twain: "Death, the only immortal who treats us all alike, whose pity and whose peace and whose refuge are for all— the soiled and the pure, the rich and the poor, the loved and the unloved." *

There were some plastic flowers laid at the base of the stone. I had nothing to leave, but I ran the tips of my fingers over the raised letters and touched the rough stone. I did not walk away empty-handed. I had found Margo and

---

Moments with Mark Twain (New York: Harper, 1920), 299.

with her, my younger self. Unfortunately, it had taken so long that it was too late to pass any wisdom down to my children while they were still young enough for it to be any use. While I was busy searching for answers, they grew up. They had figured it all out on their own and become adults. If I had neglected them in the process, they seemed to have gotten over it. As did I. We all survived.

It is not the mountain we conquer but ourselves.
—Edmund Hillary